THE FOOTBALL SCHOLARSHIP PLAYBOOK

THE STEP-BY-STEP SYSTEM TO EARN A FOOTBALL SCHOLARSHIP IN 12 WEEKS WITHOUT STARS OR CONNECTIONS

RICHIE CONTARTESI

First Edition

ISBN: 978-0-9966185-3-3

Thank You

To my parents, whose unwavering support and belief in me shaped everything I am today.

To Rose, my spouse, whose love, patience, and partnership have been my rock throughout this journey.

To my children, Carmella and Richard IV, whose laughter, joy, and inspiration drive me every day to be better.

To my incredible team at Next Play, for your dedication and commitment to helping others succeed.

To the coaches and mentors who guided me, taught me, and believed in my potential even when I didn't.

This book is as much yours as it is mine. Thank you for everything.

PLAYBOOK

1ST QUARTER: START YOUR BUSINESS

PLAY 1: THE CRITICAL FIRST STEP

"Big games aren't won by staring at the scoreboard. They're won by committing to execute just the play in front of you with everything you've got."

VINCE LOMBARDI

Every year, more than 1.1 million high school football players strap on the pads in the United States.

Of those, about 300,000 are seniors chasing the dream of playing in college and hopefully earning a scholarship.

Across all levels, including Division 1 FBS, Division 1 FCS, Division 2, and NAIA, there are only about 7,000 new football scholarships available each year.[1]

That means 2% of high school seniors will ever earn a football scholarship and only 1% will play D1.

Now for the good news, 89% of the players I've mentored using this exact playbook have earned football scholarships.

And when they follow it exactly? That number jumps to 100%.

It's the same playbook I used to earn a Division 1 football scholarship in the SEC as a 5′7″, 150-pound underdog no one believed in.

And I've spent years building on it, refining it, and testing it with athletes across the country.

Many of these athletes had no stars, which means they weren't ranked by services such as 247 sports, On3, and ESPN. Or they came from small towns, had zero connections, and were introverted or completely overlooked. But it didn't matter.

And in this book, I'm giving you that entire playbook.

Every single step. Every script. Every template. Every proven process. Nothing is held back.

You might be wondering, "Why?" The answer is simple. I want every one of the 1.1 million high school football players every year who dreams of playing at the college level—just like I did—to have a real shot. But my team and I can't coach and hold everyone accountable.

We only work closely with a select few high school football players who want to be coached and held accountable through every step of the recruiting process. But for everyone else, especially the do-it-yourselfers, this book gives you everything you need to succeed.

It answers every question, provides a proven plan, and gives you the confidence to attack the recruiting process from start until your son signs an official scholarship offer.

So whenever you feel stuck, or unsure of what to do next, this book will be your next play. You'll still want to keep up with my latest YouTube videos though.

But before we dive into what most people believe is the "meat and potatoes" of recruiting, let me ask you the most important question:

Does your son love football? I mean truly love it?

That's the first question we ask any high school player before we consider mentoring them.

Why? Because this journey is hard. It takes effort, consistency, the ability to overcome rejection, and sacrifice. If he does love it, this book will save you tens of thousands of dollars and even more time.

If your son doesn't completely love football, doesn't eat, sleep and breathe the sport, he won't stick with it. He won't do the work, he won't overcome the obstacles, and you should probably stop here. That's not harsh. That's honest.

One thing you'll learn about me right away and throughout this entire book is that I won't patronize you to make you feel better. There will be no gray area—I'll always shoot you straight.

Telling a kid he's Division I when he isn't (yet), or telling you your son doesn't need to love it to handle the rejection he'll face, would be a disservice.

This book isn't for the top 2,000 recruits out of the 1.1 million players. Those players are already being recruited by the same Power Five programs. They're ranked on sites like 247Sports, On3, and ESPN, and coaches at those schools know exactly who they are. They don't need help getting exposure, turning that exposure into interest, and interest into offers.

But here's the good news for everyone else.

Beyond those top 2,000 players, there are still thousands of scholarships at Division 1 Group of Five programs, D1-FCS programs, Division 2 programs, and NAIA programs. There are even academic-based opportunities at Division 3 schools. And for these scholarships, there is no universal ranking system. It's not about being on a list. It's not about stars. It's about becoming known.

It is literally a free-for-all, and the longer it takes your son to get known, the more other players —who may not be as talented as your son is—have opportunities to take those offers.

So that old saying, "If you're good, coaches will find you," only applies to the top 2,000 out of 1.1 million. And you would already know if your son was in that group because he'd have 15 or more Division 1 Power Five offers by now.

To earn it, you have to learn it first.

Fortunately, I learned these lessons—what's now available, today, in this book—in the hardest way possible, so you and your son don't have to.

Camps, recruiting services, and recruiting software didn't help me earn a football scholarship.

In fact, they were a giant waste of my time and money. Here's why:

1. **Recruiting Software** let me create a profile and send the same templated emails as everyone else, but D1, D2, and NAIA coaches weren't checking these sites or reading the messages. This might work if you want to go D3—but I didn't.
2. **Recruiting Services** told me they had "connections" or would send out mass emails for me, but none of them ever led to real conversations with coaches. It was frustrating

because I had no idea who these 'connections' actually were or how many athletes they were pitching.

3. **Recruiting Camps** promised to get me in front of college coaches who could offer scholarships, but every camp I attended was a giant waste of time and money. The reality was, coaches already had their guys, players they had built relationships with, or they only focused on the 6′6″ athlete or the guy running a 4.3 40-yard-dash. Even though I outplayed the so-called "D1 prospects" at my position, the coaches barely noticed.

To be clear, college recruiting camps do have a place in the recruiting process, as you will see later in this book. But only for coaches who already know you and are interested.

I was tired of waiting for my high school coach and others to do it for me. Without a plan, I felt lost.

Finally, a mentor took me under his wing. He taught me to take full responsibility for my future. So, I took control of the process myself.

Even though I signed with a Division 1 FCS program out of high school and later earned a full-ride D1 football scholarship in the SEC as a slot receiver at Ole Miss, I made many mistakes.

Regardless, parents and athletes began asking how I did it. For almost a decade, I gave basic advice. Then a serious player asked me to mentor him.

That's when I decided to create a playbook for players like me who were tired of software and services that promise the world but deliver nothing. For families who don't want to miss the opportunities I missed or make the mistakes I made.

But the playbook alone wasn't enough. These athletes wanted me to coach them through every step and hold them accountable to marketing and selling themselves.

I'm glad I did. Watching their transformation was incredible. They went from being shy, avoiding posting, and hesitating to contact coaches to becoming confident communicators. That ultimately led to football scholarship offers.

And because I was once in their shoes, I know what it feels like to be stuck, unsure of what to do next, and wanting to give up.

But I also know what it's like to have a mentor step into my life. Someone who kept me focused on my Next Play®, the next step right in front of me. This mentor helped me stop chasing the outcome, which is the scholarship offer, and instead commit to following the process, day by day, step by step, to the best of my ability.

That shift changed everything. No one believed I could earn a Division 1 football scholarship in the SEC at 5′7″ and 150 pounds. And in today's NIL and transfer portal era, it takes more than talent. It takes relentless execution and focus on the process.

But many parents and athletes get this wrong. Just like I did in the beginning.

They think the goal is to get the offer. It's not. That's your vision. The vision is critical because it reminds you where you're going and keeps you on track, but it can't be the goal.

One big reason I succeeded is because my mentor and parents praised me for showing up and doing the work to the best of my ability, not just for achieving the vision.

They taught me that the real wins are in executing the daily steps, because when you focus on just the next play in front of you, you don't quit when it gets hard. And when you don't quit just like everyone else, you will eventually build the skills, habits, and character needed to actually achieve the vision.

It's like aiming for an A in a class. Make the A your vision, but not your goal. You can't control the final grade, but you can control whether you do every homework assignment, study for every test, and show up every day prepared to give your best effort. Those are your goals. Not the A, but the work it takes to earn it.

That's the same mentality I use with every athlete I mentor. It's why my company is named Next Play, and it's also why my athletes persevere when others quit.

Too many people in general focus only on the end result, without a clear path or plan. Then fear of failure, rejection, or what others think freezes them in place, and they quit.

Players know they should post on social media, but don't. They know they should reach out to coaches, but don't. They know they should build relationships with coaches, but don't.

And at the end of each day, he can now raise his hand and say he hit his goal, regardless of the things he can't control. He can say, "I sent my goal number of emails. I hit my goal number of social media posts." And so on.

This one concept—Next Play—is the reason that despite the fact that thousands of players wanted a scholarship during my time at Ole Miss, I was the only one who actually earned one. I was the only one left. And I'm extremely grateful for the mentor in my life who taught this concept to me.

The key is committing to the process you can control, not the uncertain outcome.

So if your son makes the goal to do the steps in this book to the best of his ability, he will show up when it's uncomfortable, push through rejection, and choose action over fear. He'll learn to confidently communicate with coaches, and market himself.

These are all powerful skills that will allow him to be successful in anything he does for the rest of his life. Skills and habits that most people never build—and then they blame others for why they live an average life.

This is why I believe it's critical for young men to go through the recruiting process the right way, from start to finish, largely on their own. You can absolutely help your son, guide him, and mentor him—but you can't do it all for him.

Ask any college coach. They want to hear from the player, not the parent or handler. The parents won't be showing up to practice every day. And no one can sell your son better than he can.

Most importantly, he'll gain something even more valuable than a scholarship—undeniable confidence in himself.

Once your son learns to face fear, failure, and rejection and keep moving forward by focusing on the part he can control—his next play—he'll realize he can go after anything he wants in life. He'll trust that no matter what challenges come his way, he can overcome them. And he won't stop until he does.

That's the real transformation.

Earning a football scholarship? Believe it or not, that's the easy part. So how do we start building that kind of confidence? Not with highlight tapes. Not with random DMs. And not by just focusing on his football skills on the field or in the weight room. It starts with a commitment.

COMMITMENT

Just before the end of 5th grade, I was struggling in school. I came home from classes and both my parents were sitting at the kitchen table. When I sat down I knew something was wrong, because my mom had tears in her eyes.

My dad looked at me and said, "Your mom and I are getting a divorce." That's when the bottom dropped out. I was already falling behind, but after that, I completely lost my way.

Not long after, I walked into my classroom and my teacher asked me to step outside. I stood there in the hallway, confused. Then she looked at me and said, "I've been trying to tell you all year that if you don't make a change, you're going to fail 5th grade. I met with the principal this morning, and you've failed."

That was it. No more words. Just a wave of shame. I remember sitting alone in my room feeling like a total failure. And at that point, I wasn't even sure I wanted to be alive anymore. I felt hopeless.

But a few days later (I don't even know why) I decided to look up what it would take to play football at the University of Miami, which was my dream school. Not just the football requirements, but the academics too. The GPA. The test scores. And I printed it all out.

And after reading it, there was a small part of me that said it was possible and that maybe this is something I can do.

Huge credit to my parents, who mirrored the message of my future mentor, which was that they loved the idea of me shooting for a scholarship, or the opportunity to play at Miami. But more importantly, they loved that I had a vision and something to strive for.

Still, there were a million steps to get there. But the only one that mattered was the next play in front of me, and doing that to the best of my ability. I taped those requirements to my bedroom wall. That one act gave me something I hadn't had in a long time, hope. A target. A reason to fight. For the first time, I could see where I wanted to go, and I could start to visualize what it would be like.

From that point on, I wasn't thinking about offers or stars next to my name. I just kept asking myself, "What's my next play that I can control today?"

That was the first time I made a real commitment. Not just to a vision, but to myself and to doing the work every single day to the best of my ability to chase it.

That kind of shift doesn't happen by accident. It starts with a single decision and a powerful document I now call the Commitment Agreement.

COMMITMENT AGREEMENT

This is a simple but powerful agreement your son makes with himself to commit to executing his next play to the best of his ability, no matter what, without worrying about offers, social media, or anything else he can't control.

And it's not just some sheet of paper that gets forgotten. It's a declaration. One he'll put on the bathroom mirror and the refrigerator. One he'll see every day. One that keeps him focused when things get hard.

The Commitment Agreement Has 4 Parts:

1. Vision
2. Why
3. Expectations
4. Signature

You may be asking, "What about the goals? You said those were more important." And you're 100% right. But goals depend on where you are in the process. The next play your son needs to focus on will be given to you step-by-step in this book. But first we need the vision, to make sure we're on the right track and choosing the best next plays.

Here's how to create the Commitment Agreement and help your son own it from day one.

1. **Vision**—This is the end result your son is chasing, like earning a football scholarship.

But remember, it's never the goal. The goal is always to execute the next play in front of him to the best of his ability. The vision gives him direction when choosing a play and ensures he is always on track.

Example: I will earn a football scholarship to play at a competitive college program where I can grow as an athlete and a man.

2. **Why**—What drives him to chase the end result? What's at stake?

Example: I want to make my family proud, be a role model to my siblings, and use football to open doors for my future.

3. **Expectations**—How will he show up every single day?

We use core values for expectations to keep it simple. Use ours or write your own. These are our core values at Next Play:

- Next Play – Be coachable, accountable, and always focused on your next play.
- Learn Fast – Fail fast. Move forward faster.
- Integrity – Be early. Be in the right place. Do the right thing.
- Team First – It's always "We," never "I."
- Relentless – Be dependable and give maximum effort every single day.

4. **Signature**—His name. His ownership. His commitment.

Your son signs it at the bottom. He owns it.

Afterwards, he should tape it to the fridge. The bathroom mirror. His locker. His laptop. Anywhere he'll see it daily.

You may feel like it's okay to skip this step, but I highly recommend against it. 100% of our players that earn football scholarships do it. It flat-out works.

Consider Dennis Hail, who didn't have any offers on signing day.

But he had his Commitment Agreement taped up everywhere, and he didn't stop focusing and executing his next play just because signing day passed.

When other kids gave up, Dennis kept reaching out to coaches and marketing himself. He stayed focused. He stayed relentless.

Weeks later, he landed a D2 scholarship worth over $100,000.

Why? Because he didn't worry about the result. He committed to executing his next play no matter what.

Dennis is proof of what's possible if your son commits to the process and not just the end result.

Let's break it down now for your son.

KEY TAKEAWAYS

- Create your Commitment Agreement using the steps above or download our template for free at: Gonextplay.com/ resources.

- Ask your son the question: Does he love football? If he does, this system will transform his life—not just his game.
- A scholarship is the vision, not the goal. The goal is showing up and doing the work to the best of your ability—one play at a time.
- Confidence comes from the eventual results of consistently taking action, and never giving up. When your son focuses on executing the steps he can control, not the outcome, he becomes unstoppable.

- No one can sell your son better than he can. Coaches want to hear from him, not you. Help him, guide him, but don't do it for him.
- The process builds more than football success. It builds habits, character, and confidence that last far beyond football.
- It all starts with a Commitment Agreement. Vision. Why. Expectations. Signature. Print it out. Tape it up. Read it daily. Live it fully.

YOUR NEXT PLAY

- Fill out the Commitment Agreement together with your son. Tape it up in three places. Then come back and get ready for Chapter 2.
- This is the critical first step. And it starts with one thing: Commitment.

PLAY 2: YOUR PLAY SHEET

"If you don't know where you're going, you'll end up someplace else."

YOGI BERRA

It was the final seconds of Super Bowl XLIX. The Seattle Seahawks had the ball on the 1-yard line. They were down by four points. One play stood between them and a Super Bowl ring.

And in the backfield stood Marshawn Lynch, one of the most powerful and dominant running backs in the league. Everyone expected a simple run play to Marshawn. But instead, the Seahawks called a pass, and it was intercepted.

No game is ever won by just one play, but that wrong call at the worst possible time played a huge role in the Patriots' Super Bowl victory. That moment became one of the most controversial calls in football history. Fans, players, and coaches all over the world asked the same question, why didn't they just run the ball?

Because it's not just about calling plays. It's about calling the right play at the right time. And the same goes for recruiting as well.

Every year, I see families make the same mistakes I did and run the wrong plays at the wrong time. They try everything they can think of, sending out film, going to camps, and posting on social media without any real plan or direction. Or worse, they wait too long to do anything at all.

And just like the Seahawks, one wrong play at the wrong time can cost you the Super Bowl. In recruiting, that could be the difference between earning a full-ride scholarship or just getting a walk-on spot.

The good news is you're already ahead of most families. Your son made a commitment. And that's something most people spend their entire lives avoiding out of fear. Now, the next step is always knowing what stage your son is at in the process, so you can confidently choose the best next play.

Imagine a hardworking 15-year-old freshman shows up to his high school football practice every day, determined to earn a scholarship. His parents cheer him on. But months go by and despite his effort, no coaches are calling.

The family waits, hoping his talent will be enough. Then junior year rolls around, and suddenly, they realize they missed key opportunities in earlier years. They're scrambling to catch up, lost and frustrated.

I lived this reality and so have many other families, maybe even yours. People always said to me, "Don't worry, your high school coach will handle it," or "Just go to a few camps," or "If he's good enough, they'll find him."

But when you look at the numbers, you quickly realize that it's nearly impossible. There are about 1.1 million high school football players. Each college staff has around 15 coaches handling recruiting. That means that, for each school, every coach is responsible for evaluating more than 73,000 athletes.

So if you believe your son can just work hard on the field and coaches will magically find him, you are setting yourself up for disappointment. Unless, of course, he is ranked in the top 2,000.

Let me put that in perspective.

Out of 1.1 million high school football players each year, only 32 are ranked as potential five-star recruits. Around 300 are ranked as four-stars. And about 1,800 earn a three-star ranking.

That means only 0.19% of all players ever get ranked at all.

So if your son is chasing stars, he is wasting time. Because unless he is in the top 0.19% in the country, rankings do not come first. Offers do.

The truth is, most players do not get ranked until after they start getting offers. Coaches do not care about stars. They care about whether your son can help their team win. And after the big Power 5 programs scoop up the ranked players, there is a giant free-for-all for the rest of the players at the D1 Group of 5 and FCS levels, as well as D2, NAIA, D3, and JUCO.

You cannot just be good and expect coaches to find you. There is no way for them to find you unless you get in front of them. There is no ranking system. That's why having your son execute this playbook matters more than seeking stars.

When your son starts doing things right, the offers will come. Sometimes the stars will follow. But by that point, it will not even matter. Your son will have earned something far more important: scholarship offers.

But here is the mistake most families still make.

They assume the high school coach will handle everything. The outreach. The social media. The highlight video. And not just for your son, but for every senior. All while trying to win football games and teach classes. It is just not realistic. With that said, if your coach has strong connections, you should absolutely take advantage of them.

And I'm not saying you won't get lucky, but there's simply no way a coach can handle all of that for every senior. Plus, do you really want to put your son's dreams and success in his head coach's hands?

That's why knowing the right timing for each play is so important. So your son can take control and responsibility for his success regardless of what stage he's in.

The rest of this book will show you exactly how to run each play. This chapter focuses on when to run each play, so you know exactly which plays are most important for him to execute at each stage.

CALLING THE RIGHT PLAY AT THE RIGHT TIME

I've developed a simple play sheet that breaks recruiting down into five key stages, each with its own focus. Think of it as your recruiting version of the big glossy play sheet every coordinator holds on the sideline. But instead of scoring touchdowns, this one's for earning scholarships.

Every stage builds on the one before it. The key is to start where your son is now, then follow this playbook step-by-step through each phase:

1. Middle School (Early Exposure)
2. Freshman Year (First Impressions)
3. Sophomore Year (Visibility Phase)
4. Junior Year (Offer Phase)
5. Senior Year (Decision Phase)

Middle School (Early Exposure)

- Set up social media profiles
- Start posting football content weekly
- Study divisions and NCAA rules

Time commitment: 2 hours per week

Why this matters: Early exposure builds habits, shows consistency, and gets your son familiar with the process.

Freshman Year (First Impressions)

- Get a professional evaluation of your son's game film (Freshman, JV, and/or Varsity)
- Create his first highlight video using game footage
- Build your "big board" with 60 schools that match his current level
- Start building your brand and begin posting content weekly on social media
- Fill out online questionnaires for target schools
- Begin contacting coaches to find the coach responsible for recruiting your area and show commitment so they can see progress over time
- Begin submitting a weekly scorecard to stay accountable and track key performance indicators (KPIs)
- Attend strategic camps

Time commitment: 2 to 3 hours per week

Why this matters: Coaches get to watch how you grow. They want to see progress over time. Start now, and you build trust early while most players are waiting.

Sophomore Year (Visibility Phase)

- Get professionally re-evaluated and adjust the list of target schools as needed
- Maintain consistent outreach and content posting.
- Submit a weekly scorecard to stay accountable and track KPIs
- Create a new highlight video and send it to all area coaches you've found
- Begin selling yourself to college coaches to secure visits
- Use a system (like the Big Board or a CRM) to track school progress through each stage of the recruiting process
- Attend strategic camps

Time commitment: Spend 3 to 4 hours per week on these activities.

Why this matters: Coaches need to keep seeing your son over and over again. Visibility builds credibility. This is also your chance to start building real relationships with coaches.

Junior Year (Offer Phase)

- Get professionally re-evaluated and adjust the list of target schools as needed
- Maintain consistent outreach and content posting
- Submit a weekly scorecard to stay accountable and track KPIs
- Continue selling yourself to college coaches to secure and take visits
- Begin asking the tough critical questions
- Schedule and make phone calls
- Begin tracking and comparing offers
- Attend strategic camps
- Use a system (like the Big Board) to track school progress through each stage of the recruiting process

Time commitment: 3 to 5 hours per week

Why this matters: Junior year is the relationship and offer year.

Senior Year (Decision Phase)

- Keep doing everything from junior year, plus:
- Ask for the offer
- Adjust expectations and prepare to target D1-P5, D1-G5, D1-FCS, D2, D3, JUCO, and NAIA programs
- Make informed decisions about the best opportunities

Time commitment: 5+ hours per week

Why this matters: This is where most families panic. You won't. You'll have options to choose from and will focus on making the right decision.

WHAT ABOUT THE TRANSFER PORTAL?

One question I hear a lot from parents is, "Isn't it harder to get a scholarship now because of the portal?" It's a fair concern. But the truth might surprise you.

Every year, around 13,079 scholarships open up from graduating seniors. In 2023, 8,699 players entered the transfer portal. But here's the catch, 46% of them never found a new team.

That means over 4,000 scholarships did not go to transfers. They went to high school players.

So instead of the usual 13,000 scholarship opportunities, we are now looking at over 17,000. That is a 33% increase in available scholarships compared to just a few years ago.

The portal isn't making it harder. It's actually helping. But it only helps the athletes who know how to execute this playbook and take control of their recruiting, no matter how the game changes.

WHEN SHOULD YOU GET STARTED AND WHEN IS TOO LATE?

As you go through the rest of this playbook, use this chapter as your play sheet. It is your guide to know what to focus on based on what stage your son is in. That said, recruiting is not an exact science. The steps you take will always align with your son's highlight video, size, and accomplishments at that point.

One thing you will absolutely learn with recruiting is that it is never cut and dry. If anyone ever says, "All you have to do is…" then run. What you do next will always depend on where your son is now. There will always be exceptions that depend on your son's specific situation.

For example, if your son is starting late, just before or during senior year, you might be in the Offer Phase, not the Decision Phase.

But don't worry if you are a little unsure, as you go through this playbook it will become obvious. Or if you would like our team to professionally evaluate your son and let you know what stage he's in right now, you can go to www.gonextplay.com/evaluation.

Either way, the most important thing is getting started before time runs out. Let me share a story to illustrate this point.

I'll never forget the first time I talked to Travis Grayson.

It was towards the end of his senior year. He was a tough quarterback who had everything you'd want in a recruit, except offers.

His mom called me, stressed and confused. "Richie, I thought the coaches would've reached out by now. He's been working his tail off for years. What are we missing?"

I get calls like that all the time. A kid with real potential. Parents who care. But no traction. No plan. No exposure.

When I spoke to Travis, I could hear it in his voice. He wanted this badly. He was ready to work. The problem was, he'd made the decision to go all in on college football late. And he had no idea where to start.

So I told him the truth. "You're behind. But you're not done. If you follow this playbook and execute every play without shortcuts, we can still get this done."

And that's exactly what he did. He started doing his outreach. He followed up. He made phone calls. He learned how to sell himself to coaches. Most importantly, he was coachable, accountable, and never made excuses. He just executed.

Five weeks later, he had his first scholarship offer. From zero to a committable offer in just over a month. That's the power of going all in. I'll also say this. What Travis did is not typical. In fact, this turnaround time is still the record at Next Play.

I always say there's no such thing as starting too early in recruiting. But there is a point when it can be too late, especially if your goal is Division I.

Many D1 programs fill their classes early. If your son is not on a coach's radar by the start of his senior year, that window starts to close fast. But that doesn't mean earning a scholarship is out of reach.

I've mentored many athletes just like Travis. Some earn offers late. Some start at smaller schools, prove themselves, and transfer up. Others, like Narci Wickley, who I'll talk about later in this book, go from zero offers to Division I in six months because they follow every step without skipping.

The point is, there is still a path forward. But you have to move fast. NAIA, D2, and even D1 FCS programs recruit well after signing day. NAIA can sign players anytime. D2 programs can sign into the summer (check GoNextPlay.com for exact dates since they change every year).

In fact, some of the best opportunities show up late when other players de-commit, get injured, or don't qualify academically. So if your son is behind right now, don't panic. You're not out of time. But you are out of room to guess.

As much success as Travis had, if he had started earlier, he would've had more options. No question. The earlier you start, the more coaches know who you are, the more relationships you can build, and the more offers you can earn before your senior season ends.

And please don't fall for the myth that says, "Coaches can't talk to underclassmen, so we'll just wait until junior year." That belief holds a lot of families back.

It's true that coaches can't contact your son until the summer before junior year. But your son can absolutely contact them first. He can send emails, DMs, or even pick up the phone and call. And if he calls, the coach is allowed to talk to him for as long as they want.

Many coaches will respond, even if it's early, because they're trying to find good players before their competition does. So don't wait if you're a freshman, and don't let being behind stop you from moving forward. I'll show you exactly how to get coaches to respond, no matter where you are in the process, in a later chapter.

Whether your son is early, late, or right on time, he still has a real shot at earning a scholarship.

You just have to take it.

KEY TAKEAWAYS

- You have to know where your son is right now to know what to do next.
- Scholarships come from running the right plays at the right time, not doing everything all at once.
- It's never too early to start.
- Even if you're late, you can still catch up.
- Your son can reach out to coaches before junior year and many will respond.

YOUR NEXT PLAY

- Keep this chapter as your call sheet and immediately move on to Play 3.

PLAY 3: BECOME A BUSINESSMAN

"If You Build It, He Will Come"

FIELD OF DREAMS

There was a baker in my town, one of the best anyone had ever seen. He spent years perfecting his recipes. Every morning, he woke up at 4 a.m. and poured his heart into every loaf he made. Everyone who tasted his bread said it was the best they'd ever had.

Eventually, he decided to open his own bakery. It seemed like the logical next step. He imagined people lining up around the block the moment he opened the doors. But when he flipped the sign to "Open" for the first time, no one came.

It wasn't because the bread wasn't incredible, it was. But no one knew the bakery even existed.

He believed that if he just focused on mastering his product, that would be enough. That people would somehow just find him. Unfortunately, that belief only holds true in the classic movie *Field of Dreams*.

Now, the baker was thousands of dollars in the hole and facing a painful reality. If he wanted to survive, he would have to learn marketing and sales, skills he had never needed before. It was frustrating and overwhelming because he just wanted to bake. But if he didn't learn how to promote his business and sell, he would lose everything he had worked for.

This is the same painful lesson I had to learn. I thought if I just worked harder, trained more, lifted more, and pushed myself to the edge, someone would notice. I spent years and thousands of dollars perfecting my game. I poured everything into being a great product on the field and believed that if my highlight tape was good, coaches would find me.

But when it came time to get recruited...crickets. Just a bunch of letters in the mail and empty camp invites. And that's the same painful reality hundreds of thousands of high school football players face every year.

They grind like crazy. They build all their confidence on the field. But because they never learn how to market themselves and confidently communicate with college coaches, they have zero confidence off the field. When it's time to reach out to college coaches, they freeze. Not because they aren't good enough, but because they never built the confidence to do it.

Getting a football scholarship isn't just about being great on the field. It's about being great, getting seen, and then ultimately turning that exposure into scholarship offers.

That means your son can't just be a football player anymore. He needs to become a confident businessman.

Your son can do this, too. Even if he's shy, introverted, or doesn't yet believe in himself on the business side. I had zero confidence on the business side at first as well.

It wasn't until my mentor taught me, coached me, and held me accountable that I began to learn how to confidently communicate, follow up, and tell my story.

I started building skills, habits, and applying what I now recognize as sales and marketing skills, even though I didn't call them that back then. Those same skills and habits helped me earn a scholarship.

What I didn't realize when I first started mentoring athletes is that I wasn't just teaching kids how to get recruited. I was teaching them sales and marketing. Real business and life skills. And the crazy part is, we expect 16- and 17-year-olds to be good at marketing and sales with zero experience and no one coaching them.

Think about it. These kids are used to texting friends, not cold outreach. They're used to scrolling, not selling themselves. Yet we hand them a phone and say, "Just message the coach."

It's no wonder they freeze. It's not because they're lazy. It's because no one has ever coached them, taught them how to market themselves and sell their skills the right way.

My skills and habits helped me persevere at Ole Miss when things got tough. And years later, they gave me the confidence to build my business, Next Play. That's when I saw the bigger picture. The recruiting process wasn't just about football. It was business.

And I'd been running that business the whole time without even realizing it. That's when it clicked. I wasn't just helping kids get scholarships, I was helping them become confident businessmen.

Essentially, I was teaching business skills to high school football players. These real-world skills aren't taught in high school. But they will set your son up to succeed at whatever they choose in life. That could be crushing their first interview, or building a business. It might be moving up the corporate ladder, writing a book, or becoming a professional athlete.

One of the earlier players I mentored was a perfect example of this. When I first met him, he had all the talent in the world, but he froze when it came time to message coaches or post on social media. He didn't believe he had anything worth saying.

But after just a few months of coaching, he was leading his recruiting calls. He was asking coaches the critical tough questions that ultimately earned him multiple scholarship offers. More importantly, he began to believe in himself.

His dad pulled me aside one day and said, "Forget the scholarship. My son is a different person. He finally believes in himself off the field, too."

That's when I knew this was bigger than football. Because what he learned wasn't just how to get "exposure." It was how to run a business, his business. And the truth is, your son is already doing the same.

Whether he realizes it or not, every athlete is running a business. Some just haven't been taught how to run a successful one yet.

To understand this better, let's break down what every successful business needs to thrive. There are three core components working together: product, marketing, and sales. The product is what the company offers. Marketing is how people find out about it. Sales is what turns that interest into buyers.

The same is true in recruiting.

- **The product** is your son's game—his speed, strength, mindset, and habits. It's what he builds in the weight room, on the practice field, in film study, and through his discipline day after day.
- **Marketing** is the exposure piece. It's how college coaches discover him, how he builds his brand, and how he shows up consistently in the right places to stay top of mind.
- **Sales** is the final piece—the part most athletes overlook. It's his ability to communicate with confidence, follow up, tell his story, ask hard questions, and ultimately turn interest into scholarship offers.

Most athletes only work on the product. They train relentlessly. They lift, they run, they push themselves. But they don't learn how to market and sell themselves. They don't know how to build awareness or close the gap between interest and offers. So they end up frustrated, overlooked, and confused, wondering why their hard work hasn't turned into offers.

It's not because they aren't good enough. It's because they're only running one-third of the business.

If your son wants to earn the best football scholarships, he needs all three. Being great on the field is only one part of the equation. It's like having an amazing product that no one even knows exists. And that brings us to what matters most right now.

From this point forward, your son's mindset has to shift. He can't just train like an athlete anymore. He has to start thinking like a business owner. That means:

- He must dedicate just as much time each week to marketing and sales as he does his product.
- He needs to learn how to market himself, not just how to perform.
- He has to learn to communicate confidently with coaches, not just show confidence on the field.
- He has to follow up with coaches, ask tough questions, and run recruiting calls like a pro.
- He has to learn how to build relationships, convert interest into offers, and stay top of mind with the right coaches.

None of this replaces the work on the field. It multiplies the return on it. Your son still has to train relentlessly. He still has to earn the right to play and be a great product. But if that's all he does, he's gambling everything on the hope that someone finds him. This shift isn't about playing less football. It's about finally doing what it takes to get results from it.

And the best part? These are skills he can learn. They're not just for the naturally outgoing or the well-connected. They're learnable for anyone. Even for athletes who are introverted or on the autism spectrum.

Yes, you heard that right, I've coached players with autism and helped them develop these exact skills. And in the chapters ahead, I'll walk you through how to help your son build them too.

But before we get into the step-by-step tactics, it all starts with one powerful shift in your son's mindset:

"I'm not just an athlete. I'm a business. And it's time to start running it like a successful one."

That isn't a quote I made up. It's from a player I mentored, Felix Carillo IV.

Felix was a 5'11" tight end on a team that didn't even use tight ends. Despite that, he became the most recruited player at his school, second only to a 3-star prospect.

Let that sink in. Felix overcame surgery from an injury his junior year, played in an offensive system that didn't showcase his position, and still earned multiple offers, including a significant Division 2 offer. How?

Because he decided to treat himself like a business and went all in on marketing and sales. Players on his team who played way more than him had fewer or no offers.

His mom even said, "I am a professor at a business college, and your mentorship program was even better than my son getting a business degree."

Felix is the perfect example of what's possible when a player stops waiting to be "found" and starts running his recruiting like a successful business.

Felix's Family & Richie Contartesi - Signing Day

KEY TAKEAWAYS

- Being great on the field is only 50% of the equation. Most athletes train relentlessly but never learn how to get seen or how to turn interest into offers.
- Your son is already running a business. His product is his game. Marketing is how he gets exposure. Sales is how he communicates and closes the gap between attention and actual offers. This book shows you how to help him run a successful business.
- The best athletes don't wait to be found. They learn how to confidently communicate, follow up, and build real relationships with coaches.
- Marketing and sales are learnable skills. Confidence off the field can be built just like strength in the weight room. Even shy or introverted players can master these tools with the right guidance.
- Football is just the beginning. These skills don't just lead to scholarships. They lay the foundation for success in life, no matter what your son chooses to pursue.

YOUR NEXT PLAY

- Have a conversation with your son tonight. Ask him this one question: "Do you see yourself as a business?"
- If he hesitates, walk him through the idea that his game is the product, that college coaches are the customers, and that it's time to start leading like a successful business

owner. Not someday, but right now—if he wants to earn the best scholarships or play at the highest level possible.

- In the next chapter, I'll show you exactly how to help him do that, step by step.

2ND QUARTER: BUILD YOUR MARKETING MACHINE

PLAY 4: THE PERFECT HIGHLIGHT TAPE

"You never get a second chance to make a first impression."

WILL ROGERS

When my senior year ended I had big dreams, but no offers. Deep down, I was starting to wonder if those dreams were slipping away.

Then I received an invite. An official visit to Mount Union, a powerhouse Division III program in Ohio. I didn't want to play D3, but I had nothing else. And some big-time players went there. So I figured, why not?

My best friend was a linebacker on my team. He also got an offer to the school. So we decided to go together. I jumped in the car and drove all the way from South Florida to Ohio. It was a long and cold drive, but I was hopeful.

When we walked into the facility, I shook the coach's hand. The first thing he said was,

"Let's pull up your highlight tape." We sat down together, side by side, watching my tape. He didn't say much at first. Just watched.

Then he hit pause. Right after play number eight. He looked at me and said, "That one right there? That's the play that made me say, 'Okay, this kid can play.' But it was play number eight. Most coaches never make it past five."

Then he told me straight. "Most players have their tape in the wrong order. You guys think a linebacker going unblocked and making a big hit is a great play. But he's supposed to do that. I want to see a linebacker shed a double team and make a big hit behind the line of scrimmage. That's a great play."

I just nodded. He was right. I thought I made a good highlight video because everyone always said, "just put your best plays first." But I didn't know which plays were truly the ones that coaches were searching for. I got lucky. This coach was willing to keep watching since I'd been referred to him by another coach.

But what If I'd not had that referral? He said he would've clicked off before ever seeing the one play that could've earned me a shot. That hit hard. I just stared at the screen, thinking, how many other opportunities did I miss? I almost lost this one. Not because I didn't have the talent, but because I didn't know how to package it.

That visit changed everything. He showed me how to reorder my film the right way, and that updated tape opened doors I never thought possible. I finally started getting replies and attention from programs at higher levels, including some D1 coaches.

Talent alone won't get you noticed. If you don't learn how to market yourself the right way, no one will see what you can do. I don't want you to make the same mistake I made, especially when it's so avoidable. So let me show you the way to build your highlight tape through the lens of a marketer, not just a football player.

It all starts with understanding how your highlight tape fits into your entire marketing package.

Your marketing package includes your NCAA ID, social media accounts, transcript, and your highlight tape. This is your brand. This is your storefront. And most of the time, the first thing a coach will click on is your highlight tape.

I've interviewed college football head coaches at every level on my podcast—The Football Scholarship Podcast. And every coach says the same thing. Before a coach will offer you a scholarship, your entire marketing package has to answer three key questions:

- First, can he start and contribute on the field?
- Second, does he have the grades to qualify?
- Third, does he have the character and work ethic to fit our program?

KEY QUESTIONS YOU MUST ANSWER TO GET AN OFFER

1. **CAN HE START AND CONTRIBUTE?**
2. **DOES HE HAVE THE GRADES?**
3. **DOES HE HAVE THE CHARACTER?**

If your tape and online presence don't check all three of these boxes, over and over again, they're going to move on. One question I get all the time is: "Do I need varsity game film?"

If you want to get an offer? Yes, in most cases.

If you want to start building relationships with college coaches early, even before you're on varsity? No.

You can start marketing yourself with what you have. If that's JV or freshman tape, then use it. Saquon Barkley got his first D1 offer from his JV highlight tape. Why? Because good coaches are great evaluators. They can see talent, effort, and potential, even on lower-level film.

Coaches aren't just looking for players. They're looking for growth. They want to see how a player progresses over time. That's why I always tell athletes and parents, the earlier you start the process, the more relationships you can build. And the more relationships you build, the more offers you'll have on the table.

So as soon as you get any high school game film, get a professional evaluation. Set up your highlight video properly (like I'll teach you in this chapter). Then begin the marketing and outreach process I give you in this playbook. Start building those relationships now. Let coaches see that you're putting in the work and getting better each season.

Oh, and please don't wait until your son's tape is "perfect." I hate to break it to you, but it's probably never going to be perfect. And that's okay.

That's what the evaluation is for. Based on your game film, we can figure out which division or level gives you the best chance to play and possibly earn a scholarship. When you send your highlight video and are honest about what type of footage it is, you can start building real relationships with coaches.

If your school uses Hudl, your film is probably being recorded already. But even if your son's school isn't using that technology, it's not an excuse. In today's world, there's no reason not to have game film. You can buy a tripod on Amazon and film games with an iPhone. It doesn't have to be fancy, it just needs to be clear.

Even if you're not starting yet, even if your team is struggling, record everything. A coach may ask to see a full game, and if you don't have it, that might be the end of the conversation. Don't wait for someone else to do this for you. Take responsibility and own your process. Take control of your film. This is your business now.

Here is the 4-step system to make the perfect highlight tape like a marketer:

- Step 1: The Info Slide
- Step 2: The Hook
- Step 3: The Body
- Step 4: The Close

Step 1: The Info Slide

- **Purpose:** Create a professional first impression and make it easy for coaches to contact you. Right when the coach is done watching he can pick up the phone and call you.

- **Actions:**
  - Start with a clean headshot and basic, accurate information: name, class year, high school, height, weight, X handle, GPA, email, and cell phone.
    - Choose info that best represents you as a student-athlete.
  - Use tools like Canva.com for a clean design. We suggest Canva.com because HUDL does not allow you to use enough characters to add all the information you need.
  - Keep it under 5 seconds—treat it like an elevator pitch. No excessive details.
  - Also, add the same slide at the end for 15-20 seconds.

Step 2: The Hook

- **Purpose**: Grab the coach's attention immediately and get him to say, "I like this kid, and I want to see more."
- **Actions:**
  - Lead with your 5-6 most impressive plays—think touchdowns, deep throws, big blocks, or game-saving tackles.
    - Come at this from a college coach's perspective.
  - Keep it position-specific. Only show plays for the one position you have the best chance to get a scholarship in during the hook.
    - Don't bounce around on different sides of the ball.
    - Get a professional evaluation by an actual D1 Recruiting Director here to assess your current level.
  - Don't list accolades—let your plays speak for themselves.

Step 3: The Body

- **Purpose**: Show consistency and skill tailored to your specific position.
- **Actions:**
  - Include 8-20 of your next best clips, but quality > quantity. If you only have eight, use your top eight. If you actually have 20 or more that are actual highlights then add them.
  - Start with your best plays, coaches may not watch the whole tape.
  - Use visual cues (arrows, spot shadows) to make yourself easy to identify BEFORE the play begins.
- **Position-Specific:**
  - **Quarterbacks:** Focus on touchdown throws, splash throws (15+ yards), and mobility. Include throws on the move, off-schedule plays, and any clips that show off your athletic ability.
  - **Running Backs:** Highlight explosive runs, pass-catching skills, and physicality in pass protection. Emphasize touchdown runs, the ability to make defenders miss, and finishing runs with strength.

  - **Offensive Linemen:** Show both run blocking and pass protection. Make sure to highlight your physicality, nastiness, and athleticism—especially on plays where you're pulling or moving in space.
  - **Tight Ends:** Highlight both the run and pass game. Emphasize your pass-catching ability and blocking skills. Show your willingness to be effective and physical in the run game.
  - **Wide Receivers**: Include touchdown catches, splash plays of 20+ yards, and strong run-after-catch plays. Add blocking in the run game at the end to show you're a complete receiver. Demonstrating that you're willing to block is a big plus.
  - **Defensive Backs:** Highlight interceptions, pass breakups, and physicality in the run game. Show your ability to plant and drive, tackle in open space, and be physical in all phases.
  - **Linebackers:** Showcase physicality, aggression at the point of attack, and ability to make plays in space. Be violent and relentless. Show you can chase the ball and finish plays with impact. VIOLENCE. VIOLENCE. VIOLENCE.
  - **Defensive Linemen:** Emphasize your ability to change the line of scrimmage and play on the opponent's side of the ball. Show your power, change of direction, good pad level, and high motor from snap to whistle.
  - **Kickers:** Show your longest successful field goals first, followed by deep or out-of-the-end-zone kickoffs. Prioritize clean, consistent technique and accuracy.
- **Multi-position athletes:**
  - Include short clips showcasing your athletic versatility at the end. This is optional but can impress coaches.
  - Show your best position first and all those plays, then switch to the next position and show all those plays.
  - Don't mix and match.
- **Editing Tips:**
  - Use software you are comfortable with, options include Hudl (if available), CapCut, iMovie (Mac), or Windows Movie Maker (Windows).
  - Avoid excessive editing or flashy effects that distract from your performance. Focus on clarity and your on-field skills.

Step 4: The Close

- **Purpose**: Leave a lasting impression.
- **Actions:**
  - End with the same info slide (15-20 seconds) to make it easy for coaches to contact you right away.
  - Keep the tape concise and engaging, ensuring it ends on a high note.

HERE'S WHAT THIS PLAY LOOKS LIKE IN REAL LIFE

Kreet Makihele had the talent. But like so many athletes, he wasn't getting traction, and no one knew he existed. He posted his highlight tape on Hudl and X, sent it to dozens of coaches, and heard nothing back.

He was frustrated. And worst of all, he started questioning whether he was even good enough.

After getting in touch with us and getting a professional evaluation, we discovered the real issue. Kreet's best plays—the ones that showed he could make splash throws, move outside the pocket, and read a defense—were buried two to five minutes into the tape. Coaches never even saw them.

He had touchdowns at the beginning of his reel, but they weren't what college coaches were looking for. They looked like what every quarterback should be able to do.

So we re-ordered his film. We led with his most impressive, position-specific plays and cleaned up the design with a strong info slide at the beginning and end so a coach could call him immediately. Just as importantly, we made sure he was targeting the right schools and levels based on his current tape—not just chasing big-name logos.

Within two weeks of fixing his highlight tape and realigning his outreach, Kreet landed his first Division 1 offer—from one of his top choices. This all happened while Kreet was a junior.

That's just the beginning. As he continues to grow as a businessman, stay consistent with his outreach, and master the rest of this playbook, Kreet will end up with a lot of offers—and hopefully a tough decision to make.

I can't emphasize enough the power of a highlight tape with the right plays in the right order, sent to the right schools. If it's not built the right way and sent to the right coaches, your son will miss out on offers and opportunities he shouldn't have.

Tools

Use these tools to build a clean, coach-ready highlight tape—without needing to be a video editing expert.

- **Editing Software:** Use what's accessible and simple. Popular options include:
  - **Hudl** (if your school provides it)
  - **CapCut** (free mobile app)
  - **iMovie** (Mac users)
  - **Windows Movie Maker** (PC users)
- **Tripod for Filming:** If your school doesn't film games, take control. You can use a smartphone and a basic tripod. Use the QR code to access a reliable and affordable one on Amazon.com.

- **Design Tools:** For your info slide, use **Canva.com** to make a clean, professional slide with your headshot and contact info. Access our free canva.com slide template at GoNextPlay.com / resources.

KEY TAKEAWAYS

- Your highlight tape is your first impression, and it must be built like a marketing tool.
- You don't need varsity film to start building relationships. Freshman or JV footage is enough to begin. Good coaches can see effort, potential, and development—even at lower levels of competition.
- Coaches typically stop watching after five or six plays if they're not immediately impressed. That means you have just a few seconds to grab their attention.
- Always include a professional info slide at both the beginning and end of your tape. This makes it easy for a coach to pick up the phone and call you without digging around for your details.
- Start with your most impressive plays, position-specific clips that college coaches actually want to see. Not just what you believe are your best plays.

- Quality is far more important than quantity. Only include clips that show real potential to play at the next level.
- After you build your highlight tape, get an unbiased professional evaluation by someone with recent college football recruiting experience and has offered scholarships. I would avoid trainers, ex-athletes, NFL players, and high school coaches because it will be biased. I'm not even qualified to do evaluations myself. That's why we have a team with over 25 years of true college football recruiting experience. We determine each athlete's current level (D1-P5, D1-G5, D1-FCS, D2, D3, JUCO or NAIA), reorder the plays for maximum impact, and give clear feedback on exactly what he needs to improve to reach the next level. Whether you do it with us or someone else, that's up to you. But it is critical that you get one, or nothing after this play will work. If you'd like us to evaluate your tape, go to GoNextPlay.com/evaluation.
- Keep your tape clean, focused, and easy to follow. Skip the fancy edits, filters, or music. Coaches want to see great football, not a highlight reel made for social media.
- If your school doesn't film your games, don't wait around. Take initiative and record them yourself. A phone and a tripod are all you need. Ask a parent, friend, or teammate to help.

YOUR NEXT PLAY

- Don't wait for the "perfect" film. Start with what you have.
- Get your best current footage, even if it's JV or freshman film.
- Build your highlight tape using the 4-step framework.
- Get an unbiased professional evaluation by someone with recent college football recruiting experience. Make sure your film is ordered correctly and gives coaches a reason to keep watching. If you'd like us to do yours, go to GoNextPlay.com/evaluation.

- Get ready to start sending it to college coaches and begin building relationships.

PLAY 5: BUILD YOUR BIG BOARD

"Effort without direction is wasted."

NICK SABAN

After my visit to Mount Union, I quickly reordered my game film based on the coaches' feedback. I thought I was doing everything right. I was grinding every day. My film was sharp. My grades were good. My body was ready. I was sending out my new highlight tape. I had a vision.

But I wasn't getting any real offers. Just silence. A few more D3 invites. A bunch of "we'll keep in touch" replies and camp invites. I couldn't understand it.

I was sitting in my room one night with my laptop open, scrolling through another email to a D1 FBS school. I'd just sent my tape to them the week before. No reply. I was frustrated, angry, and confused.

Then I heard a ding from my email. I opened it and realized I just landed a meeting with a coach at Florida International University (FIU), a Division I FBS program. He said he would like to meet me in person.

I jumped out of my chair. This was huge. I hadn't received a reply before, let alone an invite. But this email was both. I was pumped. I thought maybe this was it. The breakthrough I'd been waiting for.

I dressed sharp, had my highlight tape ready, and was prepared to prove myself. I got in my car and drove all the way from Palm Beach down to Miami. I walked in with butterflies bouncing off the walls in my stomach. I told the secretary I had a meeting. She said, "Please sit down. He'll be right with you." I sat in the waiting room. Nervous. Focused.

I watched the secretary go behind a glass wall. I could see through it as she spoke with the coach. He looked at me, then turned away. She came back and said he didn't have a meeting scheduled. I showed her the email, so she went back in. Then she came back again.

"He's not going to meet with you." That's all she said. I didn't understand. He had confirmed the meeting. I pressed her, and she finally told me the truth: "He saw you sitting out here and said, 'Tell him I'm no longer interested.'"

That was it. He never even looked me in the eye. Just looked at my size and made a decision. I walked out of that building humiliated. Confused. Angry. And for the first time, I started to wonder if I was good enough to play college football.

So I called one of the only college coaches who had replied to me consistently. A D2 assistant from a smaller school. I finally just asked him, "Coach, what am I doing wrong?" He paused. Then said something I'll never forget.

"You're not doing anything wrong. You're just sending your film to the wrong schools." At first, I didn't want to hear it. But he kept going.

"You've got talent. But your size and highlight tape doesn't match the schools you're targeting. You're not behind because you're lazy. You're behind because nobody told you how to target the right divisions."

I just sat there. Quiet. Because deep down, I knew he was right. I had been wasting hundreds, if not thousands, of hours trying to get in front of coaches at the wrong divisions.

I was frustrated and even a little angry. It was a hard realization. Luckily, my mentor helped me get back up, because I was ready to give up. He said, "You can either use this as motivation or as an excuse to give up." Then he said, "Get up, and let's go get this."

That moment changed everything for me. I decided to use it as motivation. I stopped chasing schools based on what division I thought I was and chose to get a professional evaluation of my game film from a college football coach who would be honest with me. Someone who would tell me where I actually stood. Not to say I was D1 when I wasn't.

My coaches, my trainer, and everyone around me said I was D1. But they were all wrong. I'm not saying they were lying, but they weren't college football coaches with real recruiting experience.

And even if I was D1, which level? There are three inside Division I alone, so which one was it?

Division 1 football is made up of three groups: the Power Five conferences (the biggest and most funded programs), the Group of Five conferences (competitive but smaller programs like Boise State), and the FCS (Football Championship Subdivision), which is still Division 1 but offers fewer scholarships and uses a playoff system instead of bowl games.

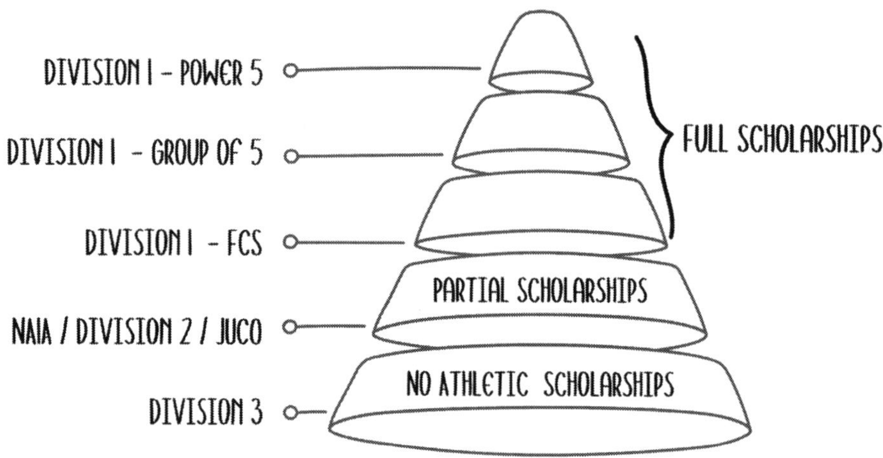

After the professional evaluation, I found out my grade was actually NAIA and Division II, with a potential shot to push for FCS if I could find one coach to believe in me. So I started targeting schools based on how I actually graded on game film. Coaches who were genuinely looking for a player like me.

Within a few weeks of realigning my target list and following everything in this playbook, I started getting replies, got on the phone with coaches who actually wanted to talk, and eventually earned an FCS offer. Not because I got better. Not because my film changed. But because I finally started targeting the right schools.

That's when I learned a critical lesson. You can build the perfect highlight tape. You can send thousands of emails. You can post on social media every day. You can go to every single camp. You can follow every step in this playbook to the letter, with maximum effort and total discipline. But if you're targeting the wrong schools, none of it will matter.

Even worse, it could cost your family the one thing you can never get back, opportunity. Once high school is over, it's over. There are no extra years. No do-overs and no second shot at getting recruited.

In this chapter, I'm going to help you avoid the mistake I made. I don't want you wasting thousands of hours chasing schools that were never a real fit. I don't want your son working his tail off for years, only to sit on signing day with nothing but silence. No offers. No visits. Just confusion, frustration, and regret.

Instead of guessing, I'm going to show you exactly how to find the right schools for your son's current level. How to match his game film, measurables, and stats to the right division. And how to target programs where he actually has a real shot at a football scholarship.

Just like you won't be guessing anymore, college coaches don't guess who to recruit either. They use a system. They build what's called a "big board."

Most of them use a software called ARMS. It helps them track every athlete they're watching. They organize players by position, interest level, and fit for their program. As film comes in, as conversations happen, and as their roster needs change, they move players up, down, or laterally on that board.

You can do the same thing.

Your son can build his own big board, a master list of schools he's actively targeting. Every school on that board should match his current level. Not the "if everything goes perfect" level. The level he's at right now.

Just like college coaches use ARMS, we use our own software called a CRM. That stands for a Coach Relationship Management tool. Coaches track players on a board and move them around. We do the same thing, keeping schools on our big board and moving them when needed.

This list should be clear, organized, and updated often. It's important for staying on top of things, following up, and using your time wisely. Knowing where each school is in the process and removing the ones that aren't interested will save you a ton of time and keep things moving.

Later in this book, I'll also show you exactly how to move each school on your big board through each stage of the recruiting process, just like coaches do. But for now, keep it simple: Build the right board. Target the right schools.

And make sure every single one is a fit for who your son is today, not who you hope he becomes later. You can always add more schools as he levels up. Let's build it.

To make this easy, I'm going to show you step-by-step how our team of college football coaches with 25+ years of real football recruiting experience evaluate game film and build Big Boards the right way for the players we mentor.

We've watched thousands of hours of high school film. We know what each level looks like. We know what each division actually wants. And now, we're going to teach you how to do it too.

Step 1: Assess Your Fit for Different Divisions

Before you build the board, you have to know what divisions you should be targeting. You can either get an unbiased professional evaluation we discussed in the last chapter, or you can do it yourself by following these steps:

1. **Step 1 - Compare Your Game Film**
   - Analyze highlight reels of players in different divisions (such as D1 Power 5, D1-G5, D1-FCS, D2, NAIA, D3) who play your son's position. You can do this by going to the active roster of a college football program, searching for a player's name on

Google along with the word "HUDL," and watching their highlight tape. Then, compare their performance to your son's.

2. **Step 2 - Compare Your Physical Attributes**
    - Measure your son's height, weight, speed, agility, and strength.
    - Compare these metrics to the standards at different college football levels online via the NCAA website.
3. **Step 3 - Compare Your Statistics**
    - Assess your son's offensive, defensive, or special teams stats. Make sure they align with what college coaches value most (such as consistency in big plays, specific skills, etc.).
4. **Step 4 - Compare Your Academics**
    - Ensure your son's GPA and standardized test scores meet the eligibility requirements for various divisions (like the NCAA, NAIA, JUCO) via the NCAA website.
    - Stats don't tell the full story. But they do help.
5. **(Optional) Attend Individual Camps**
    - Attend individual recruiting camps on college campuses where college coaches can give you feedback. These camps can give you a rough idea of what level you're tracking toward, but remember you're in shorts and a T-shirt. Just like coaches rarely offer without watching game film, you can't fully evaluate a player's level based on a no-pads camp. It's critical that it's an individual recruiting camp. (You'll learn more about those in a later chapter.)

Next Play: Choose 2-3 divisions that best align with your son's current level of play, physical attributes, statistics, and academics.

Step 2: Targeting the Right Divisions Efficiently & Effectively

Now that you know the divisions to target, it's time to get smart and make sure your son spends the right amount of time on each division. And we definitely don't want to just chase one level and hope it works out.

We want to build a list of 60 schools that match where your son is right now, not just where you hope he ends up. This keeps him focused and stops him from wasting time going after only one level and putting all his eggs in one basket.

Segment Your Target Divisions:

- **Core Schools**: These are schools at your evaluated level based on your current game film and evaluation. Spend 50% of your time targeting these schools.
- **Momentum Schools:** These are schools one level below your evaluation. They help you gain traction, stack interest, and secure offers faster. Spend 30% of your time targeting these schools to build momentum.

- **Stretch Schools:** These are schools one level above your evaluation. They require max effort and the right coach willing to take a chance. Spend 20% of your time targeting these schools.

Next Play: Now that you know your level, it's time to break it up by division. For example, if your son grades out as a D2 player, his target list might look like this:

- 50% D2
- 30% NAIA
- 20% FCS

**Please note that this isn't an exact science. For some players we evaluate and mentor, we adjust the percentages based on their specific situation.*

Step 3: Build Your Big Board

Now that you've figured out your level and split up your target divisions, it's time to build your big board. Start by choosing 60 schools that match your mix of Core, Momentum, and Stretch schools from step 2. This list will help your son stay focused and give him a clear plan for outreach.

Choosing Programs Within Each Division by Program Needs, Conference, and Fit:

- At the Power 5 and Group of 5 levels, analyze the different conferences and determine where you fit best based on level of competition, position depth, and geographic preference.
- At the FCS, D2, D3, NAIA, and JUCO levels, dig deeper. Research coaching styles, offensive and defensive systems, and current roster needs at your position. A school

might be your level, but if they just signed four freshmen at your spot, that's not the place to bet your future.

- Also consider what actually matters to you—academics, location, campus size, climate, class size, and how far it is from home. If your son hates snow, don't target North Dakota. If he wants to study engineering, don't waste time on schools that don't offer it.

Create Your Big Board:

Place all 60 schools under the Interested Schools stage to start. Here's an example of what a big board looks like inside the Next Play CRM:

Interested Schools	Questionnaire Complete	Coaches Contacted	Coaches Responded	Area Coach ID	Calls Booked	Visit	Scholarship Offer
Ole Miss	University of Louisiana at Monroe	United States Naval Army	Boise State University	Ball State University	Lousiana State University (LSU)	Vanderbilt	Georgia State University
	University of Hawaii		Coastal Carolina			Illinois	Northwestern University
	University of Maryland						Ohio University

Here are the stages in order from left to right: Interested Schools, Questionnaire Complete, Coaches Contacted, Coaches Responded, Area Coach ID, Calls Booked, Visit, Scholarship Offer.

As you execute this playbook you will move schools from left to right and lead coaches to offer you a scholarship. You can use the Next Play CRM, a spreadsheet, or whatever tool helps you track your progress. What matters most is that you use something. Because if you're not tracking it, you're guessing. And now that you have a system, you'll never have to guess again.

THE RESULT

This is about finding a great fit. It's not just about football, but finding a program that sets your son up for life after the game. When you get the fit right, everything can change fast.

The Big Board in Action

Jaidyn Vineyard came to me with zero offers and zero interest. He had talent, but his highlight tape was in the wrong order. And on top of that, he was reaching out to the wrong schools.

We professionally evaluated his film, reorganized his plays for him, and built a Big Board focused on programs where he had the best chance of earning a scholarship right now.

In just five weeks, Jaidyn went from no interest and no real conversations to landing his first Division 2 scholarship offer. And many more followed. Why? He started targeting the right 60 schools, ranked them based on his chances, optimized his highlight tape, and followed the rest of this playbook step by step.

That's the power of targeting the right schools. Now it's your turn to take control, build your Big Board, and open the door to the opportunities your son deserves.

KEY TAKEAWAYS

- Before you go any further, remember that if you build your son's Big Board by guessing his level, everything that comes next like outreach, marketing, visits, offers, and negotiation will not work. I'm not saying this to scare you. I'm saying it because getting this part right is what makes the rest of the playbook actually work.
- Be honest with where your son stands right now. Don't only chase dreams that don't match his game film, stats, or measurables. Focus on real opportunities where he can compete and grow.
- Break your target schools into three groups: Core, Momentum, and Stretch schools. Choose your schools and balance your effort accordingly.
- Research each school beyond football. Academics, coaching style, roster needs, and campus life matter too. Finding the right fit improves the chance of success on and off the field.
- It's never about talent alone. It's about targeting the right 60 programs, where coaches are looking for someone just like your son. That's how you turn hard work into real offers.

YOUR NEXT PLAY

Now it's your turn. Grab a notebook or your phone and start building your Big Board today.

- Assess Your Son's Current Level: Watch game film of players at different divisions. Measure speed, size, and grades. Know where he really fits.
- Segment Target Schools: List 60 programs divided into Core, Momentum, and Stretch groups based on your honest evaluation.
- Research Each School: Look beyond football. Find programs that offer the right academics, coaching, and culture for your son.
- Create your Big Board and place all 60 schools under the Interested Schools stage to start.
- Stay Organized. Keep your list clear and updated.
- Once more, nothing I teach in this book will work if your son is targeting the wrong schools. This alone will lead to hundreds, or even thousands, of hours of wasted time.

You can follow the steps to evaluate your son yourself outlined in Step 1 of this chapter or you can get an unbiased professional evaluation before moving on. Visit GoNextPlay.com/Evaluation if you want our team to do a professional evaluation for you.

PLAY 6: BUILD YOUR BRAND

"Care about what other people think and you will always be their prisoner."

LAO TZU

My phone rang, and when I answered, it's the parents of a quarterback from Texas. They were frustrated. Their son was talented. He had good grades. He had the film. But he wasn't doing anything to promote himself. No outreach. No posting. Nothing.

They kept telling him he needed to get on social media, send messages to coaches, and start building his brand. But he wasn't listening because he was introverted, shy, and it was coming from "Mom" and "Dad."

"Maybe he'll listen to you," they said.

So I got on a call with their son, and he had that look I see a lot, like he knew he should be posting, but didn't really believe it would matter. I asked him straight up, "Why aren't you posting?"

He shrugged and said, "I don't know what to post, and I don't want to look dumb. What if I only get one like and coaches laugh about it? Plus, I don't really think coaches care anyway."

I told him, "They care. You're just not doing anything that helps them check the three boxes coaches need to check before they offer you: Can you play for me? Do you have the grades? And what kind of kid are you?"

Then I laid it out. I said, "If you promise to post three times a week and be consistent for just a month, I promise you this will get easier. You'll get better. And ultimately, when you start doing outreach, coaches will start to respond to you."

Then to make it super easy for him, I shared with him exactly what to post and how to do it, which you'll learn in this chapter. I asked how badly he wanted to play college football. He was quiet for a moment. Then he looked up and said, "Alright. I want it a lot. I'll do whatever it takes. I'll post three days a week."

But when it was time to post, he almost didn't do it. It was a highlight clip from his spring game, a quick cut-and-go route where he threw a perfect pass to the receiver for a solid gain. He looked at the screen and thought hard about whether to post it.

He didn't want coaches to think he was showing off. Didn't want people from school to laugh. Didn't want to post something that got only one like. But he'd made a promise and knew I was going to be right there the next day to hold him accountable. So he posted it. Added a short caption. Tagged a few coaches. Then turned off his phone.

A week later, he showed up to our coaching call grinning like he'd just won the lottery. "Coach Richie! He replied," he said. "Who replied?" I asked.

"The coach from Lamar. The D1 program I was hoping to play for. I DMed him a long time ago, but he never answered. But today, he messaged me back and said, 'I've been watching your posts. You're a dog. Let's talk soon.'"

And that's when it clicked for him. Posting wasn't about going viral. It wasn't about likes, followers, or impressing friends. It was about staying on top of the coach's mind, being seen, and giving coaches a place to check you out when you do start doing outreach at a high level.

That one post turned a cold DM and a coach who had no idea who he was into an interested opportunity. And when they got on the phone later the next week, the coach already knew who he was and liked him. Why? Because he had shown up on his feed for two weeks consistently and began checking off the three boxes.

Social media lets you check all three boxes before you even get on the phone. And when you do, the call becomes your chance to close on a visit or an offer, instead of just a basic intro call where the coach is still trying to figure out who you are. I had to learn this the hard way myself.

At first, I thought I had to go viral to grow my business. I'd stare at the "Post" button and freeze. I didn't know what to say. I was afraid of what people would think. I didn't want to look dumb or be judged for getting only one like.

So I didn't post. Then my mentor said something I'll never forget, "Social media isn't about going viral. It's about giving people a place to get to know you before they work with you."

That changed everything for me. I stopped worrying about views and started focusing on just showing up and providing value. Little by little, I began to post. And little by little, my business began to grow.

Before I posted consistently, I'd get on calls with potential clients and they had no idea who I was. It was awkward. I had to prove myself from scratch every time.

But once I started posting consistently, sharing what I knew, telling my story, and teaching people how to win, those calls changed. People felt like they already knew me and they were much more ready and willing to work with me.

Just like I shared in Chapter 1, when you make the goal running a play to the best of your ability, and not concentrating on the result of the play, eventually you'll get really good if you do it consistently.

In the beginning, I was terrible at making YouTube videos. The formatting wasn't very good, and the production wasn't the best. But because my goal was just to make high-value videos and post them, I could go to bed every day knowing I hit my goal. That work was in my control.

Eventually, I got really good at making the videos. The quality was better. And I was more comfortable talking about myself so it felt more genuine to my audience. Now, my videos go viral.

But that was never the point. The initial goal wasn't to make viral videos. It was to post high-value videos three days a week.

And when I started mentoring athletes, I saw the same exact thing happen for them inside of their business. The more they posted, the easier it got. Eventually, some of their videos did go viral. That wasn't the goal. It was, however, icing on the cake.

If your son's holding back from posting because he's worried what other kids might think, he's not alone. Most athletes feel that way.

The kids who laugh or talk trash are insecure and usually the ones too scared to try themselves. Remember, it's his opportunity to get ahead of his competition and do what the other 99% of players won't do.

He can't let fear, whether it's fear of failing or fear of what people might think, stop him from chasing his dream of a scholarship. That's handing his future to someone else. Most of the loudest voices won't even be playing after high school.

But he can be, if he's willing to do what they won't: give coaches a place to go, a place to get to know him, provide a way to stay top of mind, and ultimately to earn the best football scholarships possible.

That's the real reason you post. Not for likes. Not for fame. For one thing, and one thing only: a football scholarship.

Now, before your son starts posting, he needs to make sure his profile is set up the right way. This is the first thing coaches will see when they go to his profile. If the profile is missing key info, they might just move on because they aren't able to spend time trying to find it. So keep it clean, professional, and clear. It makes a strong first impression fast.

Start with X (formerly Twitter). It's the #1 place college coaches go to check players. Once your son is posting consistently, he can begin to add other platforms like Instagram, TikTok, YouTube, and even LinkedIn (after age 16). But don't add more platforms until he's consistent on one.

Profile Setup Checklist

- Handle: Use your real name. Keep it simple and searchable. For example, @JohnSmith20.
- Profile Picture: Use a clear headshot or action shot of you in your football uniform.
- Banner Photo: Use a clean team image or action shot. No memes, cars, or chaos.
- Display Name: Use your first and last name.
- Open Your DMs: Coaches must be able to message you.

Bio Must-Haves:

- Graduation Class (ex: Class of 2026)
- Position & Jersey # (ex: WR #11)
- High School (ex: Canyon Lake HS)
- Recruiting Email (Create a separate one just for this)
- Cell Phone (for direct calls)
- City, State (Make sure you put your city, state and not just state or just city.)
- NCAA ID
- Direct Link to Highlight Video (Hudl or YouTube)

Bio Variables:

- Height & Weight
- GPA
- Test Scores
- 40-yard Dash
- Weightlifting Numbers
- Accolades
- Multi-Sport Athlete

For the variables, only add what makes your son look better on paper. For example, I am 5'7" so I'm not putting my height and weight.

Here is an example of a great bio:

Embed and Pin Your Highlight Tape

1. **Step 1: Download your highlight video** from Hudl (or wherever it's hosted). Use a free tool like savethevideo.com to download it directly from Hudl.
2. **Step 2: Upload it natively to X (Twitter)** by creating a new post on X, upload the actual video file, and publish it. This way coaches watch his video immediately and don't have to wait for ads.
3. **Step 3: Pin the video to the top** of your X profile so it auto-plays right when a coach clicks on his page.

Here is an example of a natively pinned video:

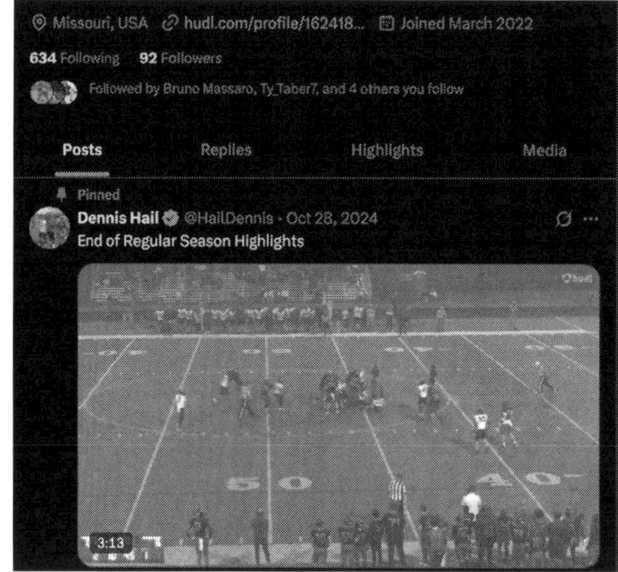

POST

Now that your profile is set up, to make posting simple and unforgettable, I teach the players I mentor a four-part framework called POST:

P – Pick Your Platform

O – Own Your Schedule

S – Schedule Your Posts

T – Talk to Coaches by Engaging

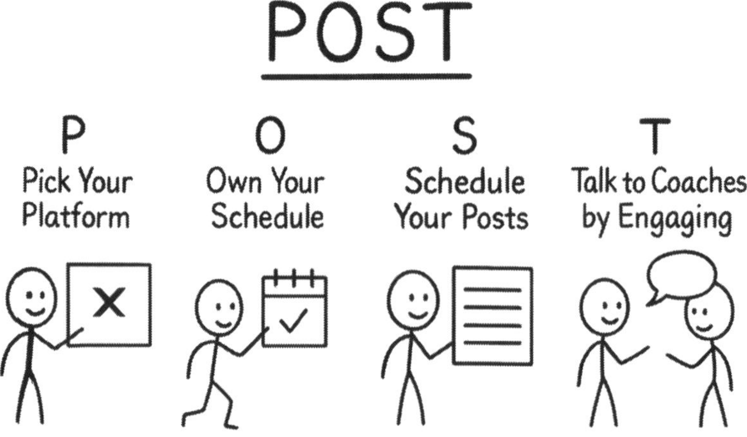

Let me break each one down for you:

Step 1: P = Pick Your Platform

Start with X (formerly Twitter). That's where the coaches are. It's where recruiting lives. Don't worry about TikTok, Instagram, or YouTube yet—unless you're already consistent and confident. Once you're posting consistently and getting responses, then you can take those same posts and share them on other platforms.

Step 2: O = Own Your Schedule

If it's not scheduled, it won't get done. Pick one day each week, block off one hour on your calendar, and use that hour to create and schedule 7 pieces of content. One for each day. Consistency is the key. You can't miss a day.

Here is your step-by-step weekly plan to begin posting consistently:

1. Choose a content day
    - Example: Every Sunday from 3–4 PM.
    - Make sure to block it off on your calendar on repeat every week.
2. Create 3–7 posts in just one hour
    - Batch your content so you don't have to think about it every day. Use the post types list to mix in highlights, academics, character, and more.

Over time you will get better and faster at this. In the beginning, just start with three posts per week. Stay authentic and consistent. The most important thing you can do is to be genuine and ensure your content aligns with who you are.

Tip: Use the same structure each week.

Your posts speak for you before you ever DM or get on a call with a coach. When a coach is watching your content, they're asking:

- Can he start and contribute on the field?
- Does he have the grades to qualify?
- Does he have the character and work ethic to fit our program?

Every post is a chance to answer those questions.

Here are the post types:

- Highlights – Share clips that show your skills and in-game and/or practice performance. Coaches want to quickly see your ability on the field.
- Work Ethic – Behind-the-scenes clips from training, lifting, or practice. Every coach wants a player who works hard when no one is watching.
- Academics – Post your GPA, grades on a test, academic awards, or honor roll recognition. Posting your grades shows coaches you're serious about school and eligible

to play.

- Character – Show leadership, community service, and just being a good teammate and person. Talent opens the door, but character gets you the offer. Coaches want leaders they can trust on and off the field.
- Achievements – Big plays, milestones, and awards. Coaches see that your hard work is paying off and that others are recognizing your impact.
- Personal – Share positive moments from your life, like hobbies, family time, or things you enjoy, to show who you are off the field. Coaches recruit people, not just players. These posts show your personality and make you relatable.
- Diet – Share pictures of healthy meals or snacks you eat to stay strong and ready for sports. Showing your nutrition proves you're committed to peak performance and long-term success.

Example schedule for beginners:

- Monday: Highlight clip
- Wednesday: Work Ethic post
- Friday: Academic update

Example schedule for advanced posters:

- Monday: Highlight clip
- Tuesday: Work Ethic post
- Wednesday: Character post
- Thursday: Academic update
- Friday: Diet post
- Saturday: Character post
- Sunday: Achievements or Personal post

How to create the posts:

Highlights

- Example: Post one play from your highlight video.
- Tip: Take your highlight video and cut it into single clips. This alone can give you a whole month of posts.

Work Ethic

- Example: Film one set of squats, bench, and or sprints from your workout.
- Tip: Record one set every time you train. Do this three times a week and you'll quickly stack up 9–12 posts.

Academics

- Example: Snap a picture of an A on a test, quiz, or homework assignment to post.
- Tip: Every report card, GPA update, or academic award is an easy post that shows coaches you're serious about school.

Character

- Example: Post a picture of volunteering at a local event or helping a teammate in practice.
- Tip: Don't overthink it. Capture small leadership moments that happen in daily life.

Achievements

- Example: Share a milestone like hitting a new PR in the weight room or getting recognized as player of the week.
- Tip: Keep a running list of big plays and awards so you never forget to post them.

Personal

- Example: Share a clip of playing guitar, fishing with family, or hanging out with friends.
- Tip: Mix in these posts to show you're more than just a football player. Coaches want to know the person, not just the athlete.

Diet

- Example: Post a photo of your protein-packed breakfast or healthy snack before practice.
- Tip: Keep it simple. One quick picture of a meal here and there gives you plenty of content.

What not to post:

The quickest way to get taken off a coach's big board is to post things that make you look bad.

- Don't post about guns, drugs, alcohol, or anything like that.
- Don't like, share, or comment on controversial or polarizing posts.
- Don't argue online or use offensive language or profanities.
- Keep it positive.

And don't think coaches only check your X account. They'll look at your Instagram and TikTok too to see who you really are, so make sure to keep everything clean.

Step 3: S = Schedule Your Posts

Scheduling your posts in advance is the easiest and most efficient way to post. It will save you a ton of time and ensure it actually happens.

You can schedule your posts using the Next Play CRM. You can also use your own CRM, or tools like Repurpose.io or Hootsuite.com, to schedule posts across all platforms with one click.

Don't rely on memory. Automate it. Set it and forget it. If you spend 1 to 2 hours each week making your posts and scheduling them for the whole week, you won't need to think about posting every day.

You can take pictures and videos during the week and then sit down once a week to schedule them.

Step 4: T = Talk to Coaches by Engaging

Eventually, you will start following coaches and when you start reaching out to coaches, they will follow you. Of course, you should definitely follow them back.

A great way to stay top of mind on social media and show you're serious about getting a scholarship at their school is by liking, resharing, and commenting on their posts. This works best if you're also posting consistently. The more they see your name, the more likely they'll reply to your outreach or contact you directly.

Here's what to do:

- Like coaches' posts
- Leave thoughtful comments
- Reshare their content with your thoughts

Engage. Engage. Engage.

Remember the shy quarterback from the start of this chapter? He was scared to post, afraid of looking silly or getting just one like. Well, after our first call, I shared this exact step-by-step plan to make posting easy. He posted that first highlight clip and got a reply from a coach, like I mentioned earlier. But he didn't stop there.

He used the Next Play CRM to save time and stay organized, posting consistently and following the rest of this playbook. He shared highlight clips, training videos, and more. When he got on the phone, coaches already knew who he was, how well he played, and were excited to talk to him.

After he got his first offer, the toughest one, he kept posting. Not long after, coaches were reaching out to him first. His hard work led to multiple NCAA Division II football scholarship offers, but he didn't stop after football season.

He was also a great baseball player, so he kept posting through baseball season too, still following this playbook. On top of all his football scholarships, he also earned several baseball scholarships, including a Division 1 offer.

This quarterback was Ty Taber, and I'm so proud of him. After working together, his parents told me, "He went from being shy and never posting to feeling just as confident off the field as he was on it." Ty himself said, "I used to hate even thinking about posting, but now I love it." He was a completely changed person. His parents added, "We were a little worried about his communication skills when he would leave for college before we worked together, but now we have no doubts at all."

KEY TAKEAWAYS

- Posting on social media is not about going viral. It's about showing coaches who your son is.
- Consistent posts on X show coaches he can play, has good grades, and is a great kid, even before they talk. Making it easy to speak with coaches when you do.
- The POST framework gives you a simple, consistent way to stay top of mind.
- Posting beats fear. Your son may be shy or scared of looking silly, but posting three times a week for a month will make it easier and build his confidence, like it did for Ty Taber.
- Share the right content. Post highlights, training, grades, leadership, achievements, personal moments, and healthy meals to answer coaches' questions about your son's skills, grades, and character.
- Engage with coaches. Liking and commenting on their posts keeps your son in their minds and makes them more likely to reply when he reaches out.
- Avoid risky posts. Posting or liking anything about guns, drugs, alcohol, or arguments can hurt his chances. Coaches check X, Instagram, and TikTok.
- Scheduling saves time. Tools like the Next Play CRM or Hootsuite.com let your son plan posts in one hour a week, so he doesn't think about it every day.
- The right post, at the right time, could be the reason a coach DMs you back.

YOUR NEXT PLAY

1. **Step 1: Talk to your son about posting**: Share Ty Taber's story to show how a shy player got offers by posting regularly. Ask how much he wants to play college football. Encourage him to try posting three times a week for one month.
2. **Step 2: Set up Your Profile**: Start with X, where coaches look for players. Help him set up his X profile with his name, position, school, and a positive photo.
3. **Step 3: Pick a content day**: Choose one hour each week, like Sunday from 3 to 4 PM, to plan posts. Sit with him the first time to make it fun and easy.

4. **Step 4: Create 2-3 posts**: Use a simple schedule from above (like Monday for a highlight clip, Wednesday for a training video, and Friday for a diet photo). Use his game film or record a lift in the weight room. Keep posts positive and true to him.
5. **Step 5: Schedule the posts**: Use a free tool like Hootsuite.com or schedule posts directly on X to plan the week's posts at once. For more time-saving options, check out the Next Play CRM at GoNextPlay.com for details.
6. **Step 6: Engage with coaches daily**: Teach him to spend five minutes a day liking, resharing, and commenting on coaches' posts. Have him comment with positive words, but not generic ones like "Great win, Coach! Good job on defense holding them to only 3 points."
7. **Step 7: Celebrate small wins**: Praise him for posting regularly, even if he gets few likes at first. Remind him it's about coaches getting to know him, not about likes or his follower count.
8. **Step 8: Rinse and repeat every single week.**

3RD QUARTER: CREATE DEMAND

PLAY 7: THE OFFER FUNNEL™

"You do not rise to the level of your goals. You fall to the level of your systems."

JAMES CLEAR

The auditorium was packed. I had just finished speaking, sharing a motivational message with a group of high school athletes and their parents. As I stepped off the stage, a hand shot up from the front row.

"Coach," the kid asked, "how the heck did you earn a college football scholarship in the SEC at just 5'7", 150 pounds?"

I smiled because I'd heard that question before. A lot. It took me back to how this all started.

After playing college football and spending some time working in the real world, I met an author who encouraged me to write my first book. He said I should share the story of how I earned a football scholarship when the odds were stacked against me.

At first, I didn't think I could do it. I had struggled with reading and writing all through school, so the idea of writing a book felt impossible. But for some reason he believed in me, and he offered to help. In exchange, I helped him with his website, a side skill I had picked up along the way.

Not long after the book launched, high schools started reaching out to me to come speak to their students. I began traveling the country, speaking at schools to inspire students and athletes to chase their dreams.

And at every stop—at more than 450 schools across the country in just five years—I was asked that same question.

Athletes, parents, and even coaches wanted to know how I pulled it off when everything was stacked against me. So I gave them tips. I shared what worked for me. But I would never see or hear from them again. I had no idea if what I told them actually helped.

Then one day, I was sitting in my office when a high school football player named Brayden walked in.

He looked defeated. He sat down, barely able to make eye contact. With tears in his eyes, he finally said, "My dad told me you earned a D1 football scholarship. Can you mentor me? I want to earn a football scholarship, but I have no idea what to do."

At first, I did what I always did. I gave him some advice based on where he was in the process. But Brayden kept coming back. For the next step. Then the next. And the next.

Brayden was serious. He was motivated. And even though he was shy and introverted, I could tell by his actions that he wanted it more than anyone I had ever spoken with. He reminded me of myself.

That's when something shifted. Up until then, I had been giving out pieces of the recruiting puzzle. But now, for the first time, I was walking someone through the entire process, step by step. I could see the pain in his eyes. I knew what he was feeling, because I had felt it too. And I knew how badly he wanted it.

So I took him under my wing. I started building this playbook from scratch, breaking it down piece by piece: what schools to target, how to structure his highlight tape, what to say in emails and DMs, what and when to post on social media.

And as he followed the system, coaches started responding. He started building real relationships and real interest followed. That's when I realized this wasn't just something that worked for me.

This was something that could work for any serious high school football player, especially the ones who had no stars, no rankings, came from small towns, or were completely overlooked.

So I refined it. I tested it with athletes in different positions, levels, and situations. I kept what worked and cut what didn't. And what came out of that process became the foundation for everything that followed.

Many athletes just send a few messages, post a few highlights on social media, and hope coaches reach out to them. They believe their biggest recruiting challenge is "exposure." I hear it all the time: exposure, exposure, exposure.

And while getting attention is critical, it's actually just the first, and easiest, problem to solve. Once you solve the exposure problem, you create new and more challenging ones, like turning that attention into highlight tape views, those views into phone calls, and those phone calls into visits and, ultimately, offers.

That's what we discovered with Brayden. We had cracked the code to get him exposure. Coaches were responding to his emails. Some followed him on social media. But everything started breaking down from there.

Sometimes we were identifying the area coach. Sometimes we weren't. And when we didn't, they wouldn't watch his highlight video. Other times, we jumped ahead, trying to get an area coach on the phone before they had even seen his video. And those calls? Total waste of time.

Everything stalled. Meaningless phone calls. No visits. No offers. Just "interest."

Every coach was in a different stage of the recruiting process and we weren't able to consistently turn attention into offers. This felt way too familiar. Before I wrote my book, I jumped into the real world and landed my first job in sales. Because that's what you do as an ex-athlete, right?

Well, it was rough at first. I actually got fired from my first job in just three months. It wasn't pretty. But at my next job? Everything changed. I finally had a sales process and a sales coach who helped me execute it, which led to becoming the top sales producer as a rookie.

That's when I learned how to build relationships, how to help people instead of just selling, and most importantly, how to follow a step-by-step sales process. I saw how much it mattered. Following a sales process and having a sales coach to guide me through it made all the difference and completely changed my results.

As I was working with Brayden, helping him navigate the conversations with coaches, I kept thinking back to my previous experience when I was going through the process and in sales.

The pressure he felt, the confusion, the hesitation. I had felt all of that in sales at my first job, but not my second one. And then it hit me, like a 250-pound linebacker.

Brayden, every high school player, and even your son, whether they realize it or not, are in sales.

They're selling themselves to coaches and trying to move coaches from interest to offers. And we're expecting young men who are 15-18 years old to just know how to do that? To be amazing salespeople without ever learning how? It's setting them up to fail. He needed a sales process and a system to follow.

That's when I realized recruiting works just like any other sales process. Just like a successful business follows a proven sales funnel to convert leads into customers, an athlete must follow a recruiting funnel to convert interested coaches into scholarship offers.

There's a clear path coaches follow before offering a scholarship. It's not just about reaching out. It's about guiding each coach through that process, where offering a scholarship becomes the obvious next step, not just a hopeful one.

Because without a plan and a sales process to follow, you're just guessing. You don't know what to do next. And when you guess? You get random results. Some good. Mostly, not so good.

And I don't want random results for the athletes I mentor. I want every athlete I work with to get consistent, predictable, and repeatable outcomes—just like I did.

That's why I created The Offer Funnel™.

After mentoring hundreds of high school football players, reviewing thousands of recruiting conversations, and interviewing many head college football coaches at every level on The Football Scholarship Podcast, I started to notice a pattern.

Every time a scholarship offer happened, it followed the same sequence. And every time it didn't, it was because one of these steps was skipped. I didn't guess these steps. I reverse-engineered them by tracking real interactions, responses, and results over time. What you're about to learn is the proven path that consistently turns attention into offers.

That was the turning point. Instead of guessing what to do next, Brayden—and now every athlete I mentor—could follow a proven step-by-step sales process that worked. One that shows exactly what stage each coach is in, what that coach has or hasn't seen, and what to do next to move them closer to an offer.

Now, no matter how these athletes meet or interact with a coach—whether at a camp, in the grocery store, over the phone, or in a DM—they know exactly what to do next.

Exposure is just the beginning. If you don't have a system to turn attention into interest, and interest into offers, then all that effort goes to waste.

THE OFFER FUNNEL™

The Offer Funnel™ is a five-step process designed to move coaches from first contact to scholarship offer. Just like in business, each stage requires a different conversation, a different focus, and a different goal.

It's critical that within each step the call to action is just to get to the next step and you never want to skip a step.

Here are the five steps:

Step 1: Find Area Coach

Determine who at each school recruits your area. This is the first contact point. If you don't start with the right person, nothing else matters.

Step 2: Video View

The goal is to get that area coach to watch your highlight video. You cannot skip this. A call with a coach when they haven't seen your video will be worthless.

Step 3: Book a Call

Once the right coach has watched your video and shows some level of interest, the next step is to get on a call. This is where the relationship begins.

Step 4: Visit

If a call goes well, your job is to move the conversation toward a visit. This could be an unofficial or official visit, for example. This is your chance to build the relationship in person, stand out, show character, and earn real trust.

Step 5: Offer

The final step is to close the coach on offering you a scholarship. By this point, you've built enough trust, proven your ability, and shown that you belong in their program.

When you understand this funnel, recruiting stops feeling random. It becomes a structured process with clear goals, checkpoints, and next steps.

So the next time your son messages a coach, runs into one at a camp or jumps on a call, he won't just be hoping for the best.

He'll know exactly what to do next.

The key is knowing where a coach is located in the offer funnel during any interaction, so you aren't guessing. If you know what stage they're in, you'll know what they've seen, what they haven't, and what makes sense to say or ask next.

That's how you stop guessing and start getting results.

And Brayden?

Once we had the funnel in place, everything changed. He knew exactly where each coach stood. He stopped wasting time chasing conversations that weren't going anywhere and started moving the right ones forward.

He ended up earning multiple Division I offers. Not because he got lucky, but because he followed the system.

That's what I want for your son too.

KEY TAKEAWAYS

- Everyone believes their biggest problem in recruiting is exposure. But exposure is just the beginning, and actually the easiest problem to solve.
- The real challenge is what comes next, which is turning that exposure into relationships, interest, and eventually offers. And for that, you need a sales process.
- Recruiting is a sales process. Whether your son knows it or not, he's in sales.
- The Offer Funnel™ gives him a clear, predictable process to follow so he can guide coaches from attention to offers.
- With The Offer Funnel™, he'll always know where each coach is in the recruiting process, and always know what to do next to move them forward. The rest of this book shows you how.

YOUR NEXT PLAY

- Draw the Offer Funnel and keep it somewhere visible while you learn the process until you have it memorized. Or go to GoNextPlay.com/resources to download our printable version for free.

- Then go straight to the next chapter to learn how to execute the first step of the funnel, which is finding the area coach for each school on your Big Board.

PLAY 8: CONTACT COACHES

"Some people want it to happen, some wish it would happen, others make it happen."

MICHAEL JORDAN

My first year at JU, an FCS program, I redshirted. I didn't play, but I practiced hard, studied film, and did everything I could to earn a shot. Then the season ended, and the head coach who recruited me got fired.

The new head coach called me into his office. I sat down, and he didn't waste any time. "Richie," he said, "we appreciate you being a part of the program, but we're going in a different direction." That was it. Just like that, I was cut.

I was shocked. I said, "Coach, you're not even giving me a chance to prove myself?" But he had already made up his mind. He said, "At this time, we are going in a different direction." And just like that, it was over.

Looking back, I get it. He wanted to build his own team. But if I'm being honest, he took one look at my size—5'7", 150 pounds—and never gave me a real chance. I walked out of that office crushed. I went into my car and just felt a heavy level of rejection. Tears poured down my face. Everything I had worked so hard for my whole life was gone.

That night I didn't know what to do, and I was dreading calling and telling my parents. I knew they were going to be disappointed in me, so I nervously called my dad. I told him what happened, and I told him I was going to quit.

He actually wasn't mad at all. Instead, he said something I'll never forget: "You can use this as a chip on your shoulder to go fight and get what you want, or you can quit like most people would. I'm not going to tell you what to do, but if you truly want to achieve this dream, all you have to do is focus on your next play, one play at a time."

After he said that, I knew I had to keep going and I couldn't give up now. So I made a decision. I opened my laptop, created a spreadsheet, and listed out all 119 Division 1 football programs, the WR coaches, and their phone numbers. Then I started calling them. One by one.

At first, I had no clue what I was doing. I would call and pitch myself, share my stats, my story, my highlights, anything I could think of. But almost every call ended the same way. Either they would ask, "What's your height and weight?" and the call would end once I answered, or they would say, "Thanks, but I'm not interested."

And I couldn't blame them. Who wants to be cold-called and pitched out of nowhere? But then a coach finally responded positively and said they appreciated the hustle, and they shared how to actually reach out the right way.

He said something that changed everything, "Before you pitch yourself, you need to find the coach who recruits your area first."

That had never occurred to me. I had just been calling the coaches at each school who coached my position, the wide receivers, and I was getting nowhere. Then another coach told me the same thing.

What these coaches were telling me was simple: find the area coach first, then build a relationship with that coach, and lastly pitch them on just the next step, which is to watch your video. That's when it clicked.

I wasn't being ignored because I wasn't good enough, I was just reaching out to the wrong person. When I started doing it the right way, starting with the area coach, my conversations got longer. My response rate went up. And for the first time, coaches started to take me seriously.

Finally, the unthinkable happened. On a long shot, I called Ole Miss. I found the area coach and he agreed to watch my film, just because I took the initiative to reach out.

Not long after, my phone rang. It was Coach Kyle. He had coached me when I was 12 years old, and again during my senior year of high school.

He said, "I just got an internship at Ole Miss and saw that you had sent your game film. The coaches unfortunately aren't going to offer you a scholarship or even a guaranteed walk-on spot, but they said they'd be open to giving you a tryout to prove to them you are who you say you are."

He added, "They really appreciated the fact that you kept reaching out, and that you did it the right way. You showed them you were serious about playing here and willing to do whatever it takes. And Coach Orgeron is looking for walk-ons like that."

Coach Orgeron, better known as Coach O, was early in his career at the time, but he would go on to win a national championship at LSU and lead arguably the greatest team in college football history. I found the right coach. I followed the process. And the right door opened.

Most athletes never even get to that point. Not because they're not good enough, but because they're either afraid of rejection or they're reaching out the wrong way, like I was at first.

In the last chapter, you learned about the Offer Funnel™, a simple process that turns attention into offers.

This chapter kicks off the first real step of the funnel, which is finding and contacting the area coach. This is the gatekeeper who can open the door to that process.

Most athletes mess this part up. They guess. They wait. They blast generic messages. They start pitching themselves right away. They write long emails filled with stats, height, weight, game film, and GPA, and they send them to the wrong coach. Plus, they use the same subject lines as every other player. They try to get an offer from an email or DM. The result? No responses. The coach just deletes it before even opening it.

I stopped doing that, and started asking one simple question: "Who's responsible for recruiting my area?" That changed everything. It made making the calls, sending the emails, and doing outreach all together, easy.

So in this chapter, I'll give you the exact system to find and connect with the right coach at every school on your Big Board. It's simple. It's clear. But first, let's break down the core problem most athletes face, and why the way they're doing outreach is almost guaranteed to fail.

THE 4C APPROVAL LADDER

Here's how the recruiting process works inside most college football programs:

1. **Area Coach:** These are position coaches who are assigned to recruit a region. If they like you, they pass your highlight video on to the position coach.
2. **Position Coach:** Once approved by the area coach, your video is passed on to the relevant position coach (for example, the running back coach). They evaluate your skills and rank you among other prospects in that area.
3. **Coordinator:** If the position coach rates you positively, your video goes to the offensive, defensive, or special teams coordinator. They determine if you'd be a valuable addition to the team and a potential scholarship candidate.
4. **Head Coach:** The final decision lies with the head coach, who reviews your evaluation and approves scholarship offers.

In some cases, once it gets past the coordinator, they all watch film as a staff every week, make decisions on whether to move to the next stage in recruiting, and start phone conversations with that player to answer the latter two questions:

- ~~Can he start and contribute on the field?~~
- Does he have the grades to qualify?
- Does he have the character and work ethic to fit our program?

If the area coach says no, it ends there. If you try to skip this step your response rate will be absolutely horrific. That's why your first goal is simple: figure out who the area coach is for each school on your Big Board. It is NOT TO PITCH your position coach.

Some smaller programs do recruit by position, and that's okay. Once you reach out, they'll tell you. But you still start with the same question: "Who's responsible for recruiting my area?"

That one question is the gateway. So instead of guessing or hoping, here's the exact system to follow. It's called The PRESS Play™, a simple process that helps your son consistently reach the right coach at every school on his Big Board.

THE PRESS PLAY

Step 1: P = Prepare—Complete the recruiting questionnaires and research the staff.

Step 2: R = Reach Out—Send personalized emails and call to find out who recruits your area.

Step 3: E = Engage—Follow, DM, and comment on coaches' posts across X and LinkedIn.

Step 4: S = Stay Consistent—Follow up weekly and keep the conversation going across platforms.

Step 5: S = Study Results—Track open rates, replies, and progress on your Big Board. Adjust as needed.

Each part of The PRESS Play maps directly to the exact actions you'll take. So now, instead of guessing, your son is running a proven route to find and connect with the coach at each school who can get him in the door to earn an offer.

Before we dive into the exact steps, there's one thing I want to make clear. Outreach isn't about being perfect. It's about taking action, even if your son is scared.

You don't need a scholarship offer to start. You don't even need game film. What you need is belief in your value and the willingness to ask one simple question: "Who's responsible for recruiting my area?"

Most players never start because they didn't get an evaluation and have no idea who to reach out to, or they're afraid of rejection. But you can't get rejected when you are just asking for the area coach. That's not a pitch. That's a question. Once your son understands that, outreach becomes simple.

When you contact a college coach using different mediums they will know you are serious and different from anyone else. When you see someone's name over and over again in different places it becomes extremely hard to ignore.

Some coaches might be more responsive to emails, while others might prefer direct calls or messages. By using different mediums, you adapt to their communication preference and skyrocket your response rate.

Now here's how to find the area coach, step-by-step. We start with simple questionnaires.

Step 1: P = Prepare—Complete the recruiting questionnaires and research the staff.

A college football recruiting questionnaire is a form that colleges and universities use to learn more about students who are interested in being a part of the program.

Filling it out doesn't mean your son is done. Most schools get 500 to 3,000 of these forms every year. This is just the beginning. It's a filter for them, but it's a tool for him. It shows coaches he is serious, and it increases his chances of getting a response later.

Here's exactly what to do:

1. Go to each school's athletics website and find their recruiting questionnaire. (Or use the Next Play CRM, where we link every school's questionnaire in one place.)
2. Fill out every question carefully. Then save your answers in a Word doc.
3. Use that doc to copy and paste your answers into other schools' questionnaires so you don't have to retype everything. Efficiency at its finest.
4. Then move the school to the next stage on your Big Board: Questionnaire Complete.

We talked earlier about building your son's big board. Now it's time to use it. Here's a reminder of what a big board looks like:

Interested Schools	Questionnaire Complete	Coaches Contacted	Coaches Responded	Area Coach ID	Calls Booked	Visit	Scholarship Offer
Ole Miss	University of Louisiana at Monroe	United States Naval Army	Boise State University	Ball State University	Lousiana State University (LSU)	Vanderbilt	Georgia State University
	University of Hawaii		Coastal Carolina			Illinois	Northwestern University
	University of Maryland						Ohio University

As you follow the steps in this chapter, you'll move schools forward from one stage to the next: Interested Schools → Questionnaire Complete → Coaches Contacted. Remember, you're not just guessing anymore. You're running a system. You have 60 schools. Here's an example of what it looks like when just one of them, like Ole Miss, moves from "Interested School" to "Questionnaire Complete."

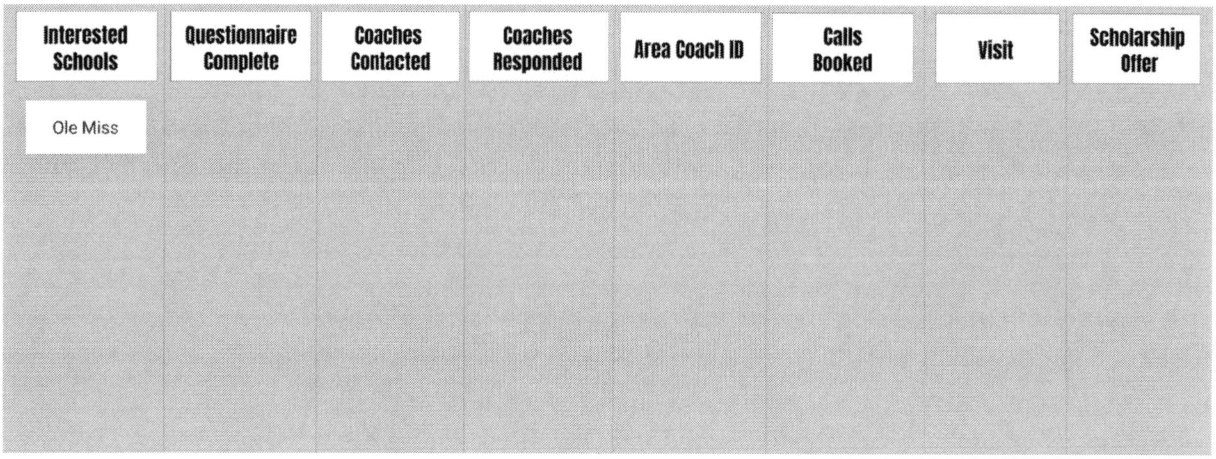

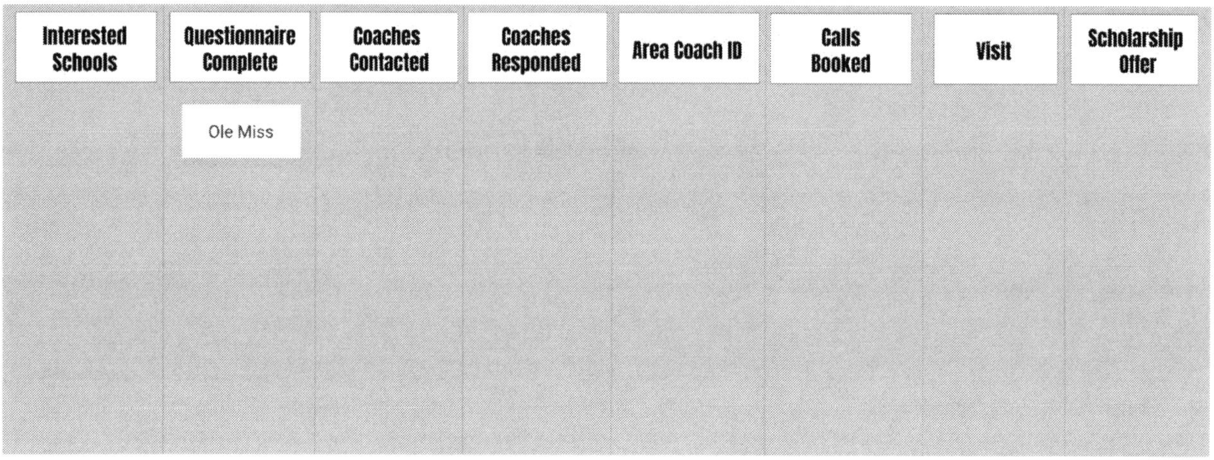

Interested Schools	Questionnaire Complete	Coaches Contacted	Coaches Responded	Area Coach ID	Calls Booked	Visit	Scholarship Offer
Ole Miss							

Interested Schools	Questionnaire Complete	Coaches Contacted	Coaches Responded	Area Coach ID	Calls Booked	Visit	Scholarship Offer
	Ole Miss						

** Important: This shows initiative. It also gives coaches an easy way to keep track of you. It's not enough, but it's a required first step. Fill out the questionnaire first so when you send your email and mention you already did it, your response rate goes up.*

After you complete the questionnaire and in preparation for step 2, you need to find the right coaches to contact. That means getting their email address and sometimes their phone number too.

The secret that no one knows about is that every public college and university is legally required to list staff email addresses somewhere on their website, even if they don't list them on the football team's staff page.

Here's how to find them:

1. Check the football staff page first. Some schools make it easy and list emails and numbers right there.
2. If not, go to the school's main website and search for the "staff directory." That's where you'll usually find emails for football staff, recruiting assistants, football ops, and grad assistants.

3. Still can't find it? Google the coach's name + school name + "email." That will usually bring up their bio or a contact page.

Over time, our team ended up building a tool into the Next Play CRM using automation and AI to collect and organize every coach's contact info so it stays updated and saves us time. But even if you're doing this on your own, just remember, the info is out there. It just takes a little digging and patience.

Once your son has completed all the questionnaires and gathered the contact info, now you're ready for Step 2.

Step 2: R = Reach Out—Send personalized emails and call to find out who recruits your area.

- To find the area coach you must email every coach on staff except the head coach, OC, and DC—Unless it is an NAIA or D3 program. For smaller programs you will email everyone.
- Make sure to also email the person in each one of these roles: Player Personal, Recruiting Coordinator, Player Development, Football Operations, Director of On-Campus Recruiting, Graduate Assistants and the General Manager. Your sole mission in the beginning is to figure out who the area coach is for each school. And the people in these positions either know or can find out for you. Usually are also more apt to reply.
- Remember, your only goal is to find out who is responsible for recruiting your area. You are not pitching yourself yet.
- Make sure to add a personalized line from their bio or stats (see example below).
- Subject line = name of the school the coach works for. That's it. Simple works. We've tested a lot of subject lines and that has the highest open rate.
- Then move the school to the next stage on your big board:

Interested Schools	Questionnaire Complete	Coaches Contacted	Coaches Responded	Area Coach ID	Calls Booked	Visit	Scholarship Offer
		Ole Miss					

Area Coach Email Template:

Subject: (Target School Name)

Coach (Last Name),

I hope you are doing well. (Insert Personalized Line from their bio or stats.)

Who would be the coach responsible for recruiting (Your City, State)?

I completed the recruiting questionnaire as well. I really appreciate your response.

Email Signature

- (Your Name)
- *(Link to your film if it is after June 15 of your son's junior year.) If you are younger, do not link your film or put your class year, because coaches can't respond. If you don't put it in the email, they are much more likely to respond.*

Personalized line example:

If I were contacting coach Kane Ioane, I would google his name and the school.

Here is some information I found from his bio on their website: The Broncos allowed just 19.0 points per game to opponents during the 2021 season, ranking 12th nationally, and with 23 turnovers in 12 games, the defense ranked tied for 21st nationally in the statistical category, registering the most turnovers since 2012 when the team recorded 29.

Here is how I would craft the personalized line: *"Congrats on only allowing 19 points per game and having 23 turnovers in 12 games. I am a turnover machine so I had to reach out".*

The personalized line is what makes or breaks your response rate. We've tested it a lot and have sent tens of thousands of emails, and the athletes who personalize their emails get over 6X more replies. Copy and paste a generic blast, and your response rate will be in the gutter. Here's an example of a real reply one of the players I mentor received from a Division I coach just because they added a personalized line:

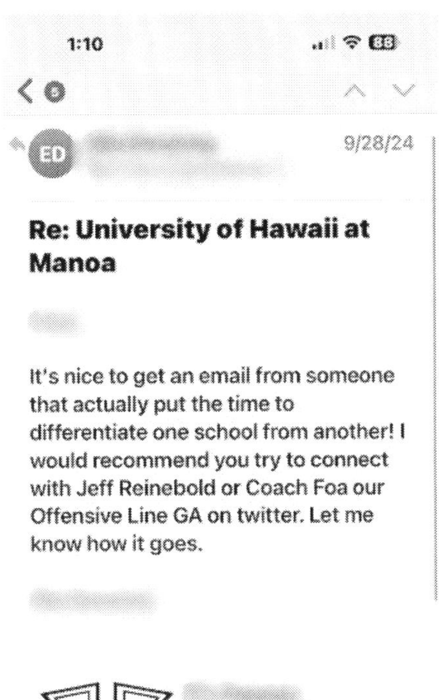

1:10

9/28/24

Re: University of Hawaii at Manoa

It's nice to get an email from someone that actually put the time to differentiate one school from another! I would recommend you try to connect with Jeff Reinebold or Coach Foa our Offensive Line GA on twitter. Let me know how it goes.

Call and Leave a Voicemail

- You call every coach just like you do via email.
- Same message as the email so you should have no fear. You aren't selling anything. You are just calling to find out who is recruiting your area so you can send your highlight video.
- Tonality Matters so be clear, confident, and respectful.
- You can find their phone numbers in the Next Play CRM or on the team's website. Some schools do not have phone numbers and in that case you can do some digging or skip this step.
- Make sure to role-play this with your mentor or parents at least 15-20 times before starting.

Call Script:

Hi Coach (Last Name), this is (Your Name). I hope you are doing well. I'm a high school football player from (Your City, State). Who would be the coach responsible for recruiting (Your City, State)?

Voicemail Script:

Hi Coach (Last Name), this is (Your Name) I hope you are doing well. I'm a high school football player from (Your City, State). Who would be the coach responsible for recruiting (Your City, State)? If you could give me a quick call or just text me at (Your Number), I'd really appreciate it. Thank you!

How Much Outreach Is Enough?

One of the most common questions I get from parents is, "How much outreach should my son actually be doing each week?"

Well, if you want real results, you need real volume. A good benchmark is 100–200 personalized messages per week.

That might sound like a lot, but remember, recruiting is a numbers game and consistency matters more than anything else.

You can make this more manageable by time-blocking 1 hour each day specifically for outreach. During this time, send messages. Also, as you can see below once you get going you can use AI and automation to add fuel to the fire.

Step 3: E = Engage—Follow, DM, and comment on coaches' posts across X and LinkedIn.

- Friend the coach on Linkedin.
- Follow the coach on X.
  - What's great about following is if the coach follows back they will start getting indoctrinated by the content that you post.
- After following, immediately start engaging with their posts.
  - Like their updates / posts.
  - Leave real, genuine, and thoughtful comments (avoid generic ones like "great post").
  - Share their posts when it makes sense.
- Then send the same message from your email as a DM.
- Do this on both X and LinkedIn.
- For faster results, record a selfie-style video and say the same script and send that as a DM if you really want to increase your response rate. We found this to increase responses in some cases by over 45%.

Video Message Script:

Hold up your phone selfie style and literally just read the phone script from the previous lesson. You can download a free teleprompter app as well if that helps you. Just look into the camera and say:

Hi Coach (Last Name), my name is (Your Name). I'm a high school football player from (Your City, State). I am really interested in (School Name). Who would be the coach responsible for recruiting (Your City, State)? If you could shoot me a quick reply, it would mean a lot. Thank you!

Sending a video and customizing it shows that it isn't just a generic message. Keep it natural. Smile. Be respectful and confident.

Step 4: S = Stay Consistent—Follow up weekly and keep the conversation going across platforms

- This is an extremely critical step. Most athletes will never follow up, while 75% or more of your responses will come from the follow-up. Here is an example of an SEC coach finally responding positively to the 5th follow-up:

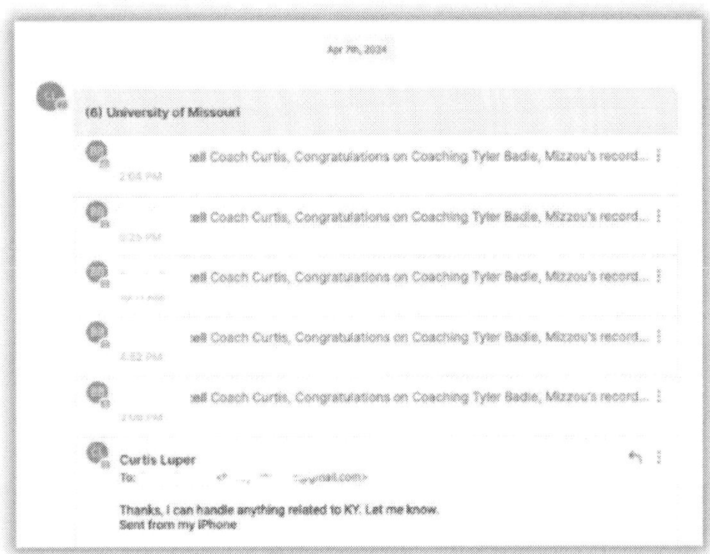

- After each message, call, or DM, create a task to follow up in one week in the Next Play CRM or in any task management system you use. A tool like todoist.com will also work.
- Send five follow-ups total. Each one spaced one week apart.
- The follow-up message is the exact same message as the original one. Just copy and paste.
- It is critical that each follow-up is in the same email thread. Do not create a new email each time.
- For X, Unfollow and then follow each account again, engage with their content, and then send your follow-up. The repeated follow/unfollow strategy ensures your profile stays visible.
- If still no reply:
  - And you are younger than a junior, wait 1–2 months and restart.
  - And if you are older than a junior, wait 1–2 weeks and then go right into sending your pitch, which you will learn how to do in the next chapter.
- Follow the same process again.

Follow-Up Tip: If you still haven't received a response you can always ask: Did you receive my questionnaire?

Step 5: S = Study Results—Track open rates, replies, and progress on your Big Board. Adjust as needed.

Use this system to stay focused and make smart adjustments to your outreach.

Key Performance Indicators (KPIs) to track and hit for this step:

Here are the most important KPIs for this step to track

- Emails Sent
- Opens
- Open Rate (Goal - 50%+)
- Responses
- Response Rate (Goal - 8%+)

	EMAILS SENT	OPENS	OPEN %	RESPONSES	RESPONSE %
	100	50	50%	5	10%
	100	60	60%	8	13%
	80	50	62%	4	8%

If your open rate is low, here are a few potential challenges:

- Your email may be going to spam. Use an email warm-up tool like www.warmupinbox.com or the Next Play CRM to help prevent this before you start sending cold emails. These tools work by sending, opening, and clicking links in emails from your new account to show your provider that your emails are legitimate. This helps them land in the inbox instead of spam.
- Make sure the school name is spelled right and looks clean.

If your response rate is low, here are a few potential challenges:

- Improve your personalized line. It may still look too generic.

- Email schools that match your highlight video. If you email schools that aren't in the divisions matching your game film, coaches will click and watch your highlight video but not respond.

If you're not finding the area coach, here are a few potential challenges:

- Make sure you're emailing everyone on the staff in the football department.
- Follow up every week consistently at least five times.
- Make sure all your follow-ups are in the same email thread.

Step 6: Add Fuel to the Fire with AI Automation

After you've tracked your outreach, made adjustments using the KPIs, and dialed in your messaging and follow-ups, now it's time to add fuel to the fire.

We built a tool that uses AI to generate a personalized line for every coach.Then it automatically sends an email, follows the coach on X, and sends a matching DM. It also follows up in the same email and DM thread three to five times, depending on the coach.

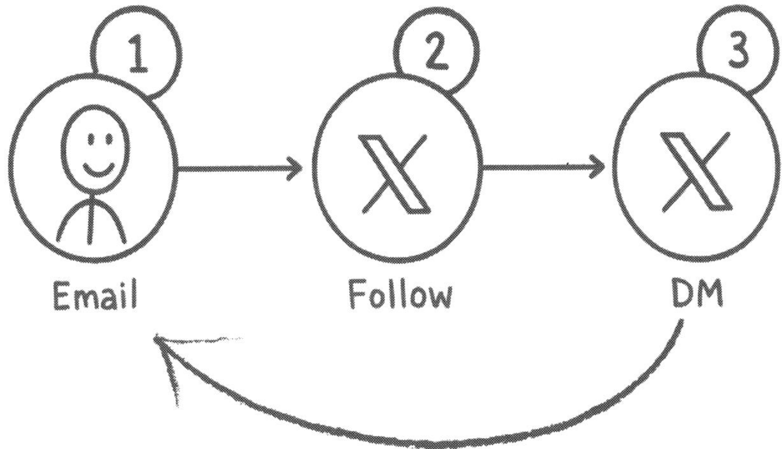

The best part? It listens. If the coach replies to the email, the DMs stop. If they reply to the DM, the emails stop. It's smart, personal, and incredibly efficient.

Once your son learns how to do and optimize outreach, automation gives him his time back and multiplies what is already working. That matters, because when the responses start coming in, and they will, his focus needs to shift from chasing attention to building strong relationships with coaches.

BONUS STEP: The Warm Market Play

If your son already knows players at the college level including former teammates, friends, or family connections, then this play can give you a jumpstart. It's a simple way to leverage existing relationships without coming across as pushy or asking for handouts.

Step 1: Build Your List

- Identify everyone you know who is currently playing college football.
- Focus on those playing at schools you're interested in and that fit your level of play.
- Time-block 45 minutes to brainstorm names of old teammates, friends, family connections, and coaches.

Step 2: Send Messages and Follow Up

- Reach out with a simple, personalized message asking for advice, not favors.
- If they don't reply, follow up one week later.

"Name, congrats on playing at [School] and achieving [specific accomplishment]. I was wondering if I could get some advice from you? It would really mean a lot to me."

Step 3: Once They Respond

- Push to schedule a quick call:

"Name, I really appreciate that. When is a good time for a quick call?"

- On the call, ask for advice first, then make your ask:

"I'm doing everything I can to play college football. How do you suggest I do outreach?"

"Would you share my tape with your coach or introduce me?"

"Would it be okay if I followed back up with you in a few weeks?"

This simple play can accelerate your outreach by getting your son's name and film in front of the right people faster from people you may already know.

You've seen the system. You've seen how to run The PRESS Play and move schools down your Big Board. Now, here's what it looks like in real life.

THE POWER OF CONSISTENT OUTREACH

Blake Steed should've been counted out. He got into a head-on car accident and then missed his entire senior season with an injury.

No new film. No recent stats. No momentum. But Blake did what most athletes won't: he showed up anyway.

While most players would've waited, or worse, quit, Blake locked in on his Next Play. He followed this exact outreach process. Week after week and even without senior film.

He didn't beg. He didn't pitch his past. He just asked the question: "Who's responsible for recruiting my area?"

He tracked his schools on his Big Board. And most importantly, he stayed consistent. Blake couldn't control his injury, but he took full control of the business side of recruiting. That's what opened the door.

Eventually, after following this entire playbook and adding fuel to the fire, a college coach gave him a shot. Not just because of his film, but a combination of his film and how he carried himself through adversity. His character, his discipline, his follow-through.

Blake earned a football scholarship without playing a single snap his senior year. That moment changed everything for me. From that point on, I knew no athlete I mentor could ever say, "I can't." No excuses.

Blake's Family & Richie On Signing Day

As for the opportunity at Ole Miss? They didn't promise me anything. No guaranteed walk-on. No scholarship. Just a tryout. But after everything I'd been through, I didn't need a promise. I needed a door. And when I found it, I kicked it open.

KEY TAKEAWAYS

- Your son's goal is not to pitch himself in a long email or DM and get an offer right away, it's to identify the area coach and start building a relationship.
- Skipping the area coach is the #1 reason athletes get ignored. (You must be targeting the right divisions though based on your game film)
- You're not bothering coaches, you're giving them a reason to pay attention.
- Rejection is part of recruiting. It's not failure, it's feedback. Treat every "no" like a first down, not a turnover.
- The athletes who win are the ones who stay consistent and track their progress. Outreach is a long game, not a one-and-done move.
- Trust the system. Follow the PRESS Play. And remember: the first offer is always the hardest, but it's also the one that changes everything.

YOUR NEXT PLAY

- Write the PRESS Play and 4C Recruiting Ladder on a sticky note, or download and print them for free at gonextplay.com/resources, and put them on your computer or phone.

- Start outreach immediately. Begin by filling out questionnaires for all the schools on your Big Board.
- Then follow the PRESS Play to reach out to the coaches at those schools.
- Track your progress using your Big Board. Every action moves a school forward.
- Put down the book and do outreach until you've gotten a response. It's time to take action. Once you've received your first reply, come back and read the next chapter.

PLAY 9: SELL YOURSELF

"Do today what others won't, so tomorrow you can have what others don't"

JERRY RICE

I packed up everything I owned in South Florida and drove 13 hours to start over in Oxford, Mississippi, all for one tryout. One shot. That was all I had. I didn't know a single person in the entire state except for Coach Kyle. As I drove down Manning Way, my heart was racing.

When I walked into the indoor practice facility, I couldn't believe my eyes. This was my dream. But I only had one shot to prove that I belonged at Ole Miss.

I sat down on the floor, laced up my cleats, and tried to calm my nerves. My heart was pounding out of my chest. But in that moment, I heard my mentor's voice and my parents' encouragement echoing in my head. They always reminded me, "Just focus on your next play. One play at a time."

So I did exactly that. I focused on doing the stretches to the best of my ability. Then I gave everything I had during the warm-up. After that, I locked in on running the cleanest, sharpest route I could. Then I focused on the ball and caught it like everything depended on it.

I made sure I was always leading from the front of the line, hustling from drill to drill, and keeping my attention on one thing, my next play. After the tryout, I left the field unsure of how I did. My mind kept going back and forth. Did I do enough? Did I blow it?

Eventually, my phone rang. I answered, and my heart pounded all over again. Was this the call that would change my life? Then I heard the one thing I feared most.

"We're going in a different direction."

In that moment, I thought it was over. I had already been cut from an FCS program. I had gone all in on Ole Miss, and now I couldn't even make the team as a walk-on. It felt like the dream was gone.

I picked up the phone and called my dad, just like I did after JU. I was hoping he would let me make an excuse and give me a way out. But just like before, he said the same thing he always did: "You can quit like everyone else, or you can focus on the next play."

I was so frustrated I felt like ripping the hair out of my head. I had every excuse to pack up and go home. But in that moment, I made a decision. I didn't move my entire life and drive 13 hours to Oxford, Mississippi just to give up. Deep down, I knew I had to do one of the hardest things a person can do. I had to sell myself.

I had no idea how to do this the right way so I called my mentor. I told him everything, how I felt like a failure, how I wanted to quit, how I didn't know what to say.

He said, "Richie, you don't need to convince the coaches to give you a scholarship or even a roster spot. You just need to sell them on the next step. Just ask for a week to prove yourself." I said, "That's it? Without a roster spot, what am I even going to do?" He said, "Prove yourself. You have to make it easy for them to say yes."

Then he shared exactly what I needed to say. We role-played the conversation over and over again until I could say it with confidence. That call gave me the clarity, the words, and the courage to do what I had to do next.

I walked to the coaches' offices with my palms sweating. I sat outside for almost an hour, going back and forth in my mind. I was about to walk in, then I wasn't ready. I'd stand up to open the door, then sit back down. Finally, I stood up, took a deep breath, and walked into the building.

I made my way to the coach's office, looked him in the eyes, and said, "Coach, I understand why you decided to go in a different direction. I'm not here to beg for a guaranteed roster spot, and I'm not saying I'll ever even play in a game here. But what I can guarantee is that I will make your defense better. Just give me one week to prove that I can take the hits and show you that I can make your defense better by being on the scout team. That's it. Just one week to prove it."

He leaned back in his chair with his arms crossed and sat in silence for what felt like the longest 30 seconds of my life. Then he said, "Richie, you moved all the way up here from Florida. You did well at the tryout, but we thought you were undersized and wouldn't be able to take the hits. But you had the guts to come into my office. You didn't pitch me on a roster spot. You just asked for an opportunity to prove yourself. So I'm going to give you that shot. You've got one week. And you better prove me right, or the other coaches are going to be all over me."

I walked out of that office and joy surged through my chest, down my spine, and up through the top of my head. I was going to get the chance to live my dream and play Division I college football.

That experience reinforced one of the most powerful lessons I ever learned from my mentor about sales. You don't sell the final product on the first call. You don't ask someone to marry you on the first date. And you don't try to get a coach to offer you everything in the first message or phone call. You make it about them, not you. You show how you can help them succeed, like making their offense better, and you focus on selling just the next step. One step at a time.

That mindset not only helped me earn an FCS offer out of high school, but it also helped me earn the one-week shot at Ole Miss. Ultimately, that one week turned into a roster spot and that roster spot turned into a role on the scout team.

Looking back, I just wish I had learned these two lessons earlier. If I had known how to sell the next step, how to communicate my value to a coach, and how to handle rejection back in high school, I believe I would've signed with a much better school. That's exactly why I do what I do now so your son doesn't have to learn it the hard way like I did.

The second big lesson I learned is that the hardest thing to sell is yourself, but no one can do it better than you can. No handler, recruiting service, or even a parent can step into a coach's office and sell your son better than your son can.

The reason it's so hard is because rejection cuts deeper when it's personal. When you're selling a product or a service and someone says no, it still hurts, but it's not the same as when they say no to you. It's much easier to avoid that kind of pain altogether.

It would have been easier to never walk into the coach's office and just blame the end of my football career on my height. Everyone would have believed me. Or, as a recruit, to avoid calling the coach or skip sending the email because you don't want to risk hearing "no."

It feels safer to tell yourself "I'm just not good enough," do nothing, and stay comfortable like everyone else. But after all the dust settles, I know deep down I would have had to live the rest of my life asking, what if?

These two lessons, learned through the recruiting process, didn't just help me achieve my dream. They helped me thrive in business, too.

As a professional speaker, I booked many large events. Yes, I spoke at over 450 schools and at major national corporate conferences, including IBM, HP, and NRG Energy, just to name a few.

Richie Contartesi Speaking

But don't get me wrong, there were plenty of times organizations emailed back and said, "We decided to go with a different speaker." That kind of rejection still stung. But the experience at Ole Miss gave me the mental strength to handle it.

Your son is going to face rejection too. Not just in recruiting, but throughout his entire life. He'll face it when a job application gets turned down. He'll feel it when a girl he loves chooses someone else. And when the rejection is personal, when it's him being told he's not good enough, that's the hardest kind to face.

But learning how to handle it now will give him an edge most people never develop. Rejection won't hold him back. It will build him up.

When he follows the process outlined in this playbook and stays consistent, it becomes easier. That's also why we don't want to target just a few schools. If all your eggs are in one basket and that basket says no, there's nothing left. But if you target 60 schools, there's always another opportunity. Rejection doesn't become the end. It becomes part of the journey, and another opportunity to get better.

When I started Next Play, it happened again. Today we have tons of case studies and even a waitlist. But I built the program from scratch, so in the beginning, every "no" felt personal. Every time someone said, "We're going in a different direction," it felt just like being back in that locker room, hearing the words, "You didn't make the team."

But I kept going. I'd faced that kind of rejection so many times, and with my mentor's help, I learned how to handle it. Failing to get past rejection is one of the biggest reasons why so many businesses fail in the first few years. But we didn't. We thrived. Every offer I've ever earned—whether on the field, on a stage, or in business—came from just selling the next step.

Give me one week. Watch this video. Let's get on a call. Let me prove it.

These same lessons and mindset are what I teach the athletes I mentor today. They understand that selling yourself is the hardest part of recruiting and that they will face rejection. But no one else can do it better.

This process works. Even if you're shy. Even if you're an introvert. Even if you have no confidence right now. Selling yourself isn't about being loud or flashy. It's about being consistent, clear, and confident in who you are and what you bring to the table.

Some athletes tell me, "But I'm humble. I don't want to come across like I'm bragging." I get it. But here's the truth. Real humility isn't staying silent, real humility is being willing to speak up and serve a team that you believe you can help. Coaches can't recruit players they never hear from. Staying quiet doesn't make you humble. It just keeps you invisible.

When a coach doesn't respond to an email, it's frustrating. But when they look you in the eye and say you're not what they're looking for, it hits differently. That's why I coach and mentor athletes through it. I prepare them to face rejection and keep moving forward in recruiting, and in life.

Those two lessons changed everything for me. First, just sell the next step by leading with value. Second, no one can sell you better than you can.

But to do that, you have to know what to say. And part of knowing what to say is knowing how to tell your story. Because that's what a great pitch really is, a personal story that shows who you are, how you help the team, and why you belong. Your son's story will change as he grows, and he needs to know how to update it and communicate it clearly every step of the way.

Most athletes get this part completely wrong. They send long messages that look like everyone else's and coaches ignore them. Or worse, they say nothing at all because they don't know where to start.

That's exactly why I created the system in this chapter.

Because what I learned from that call with my mentor and later in business and sales is the same lesson I've taught every athlete I've mentored since. That lesson has helped 89% of them earn football scholarships. When you follow a proven pitch structure that sells only the next step and focuses on helping the coach, not begging for an offer, everything changes.

And that system is called…

THE PERFECT PITCH™ FRAMEWORK

Congratulations. You received your first response and identified your first area coach. This is the part of The Offer Funnel™ where you focus on getting the coach to watch your highlight video.

Coaches are busy and get hundreds of messages, so the only goal of your pitch is to get them to watch your highlight film and take the next step. Don't try to sell them on a full scholarship right away.

Everyone else sends the same email with the same subject line like what you see below:

- 5'10" Running Back, Class of 2026: Marcus Johnson, Atlanta GA, Full Game Film
- Linebacker Prospect: 2025 Grad, 3.7 GPA, 300 Bench, 4.6 Forty, Contact Me
- 6'2" Quarterback, Class of 2027: Jake Swift, Dallas TX, See Highlights
- Wide Receiver Recruit: 6'1", Class of 2027, Michael Brown, Houston TX, Hudl Link

They pack in so much information trying to get an offer on the first try. But coaches know exactly what to look for, and when they see one of those messages, they either delete it right away or toss it in a folder to "review later," which never actually happens. You know exactly the kind of email I'm talking about. It's the same type everyone sends like you can see below. This is what you don't want to do:

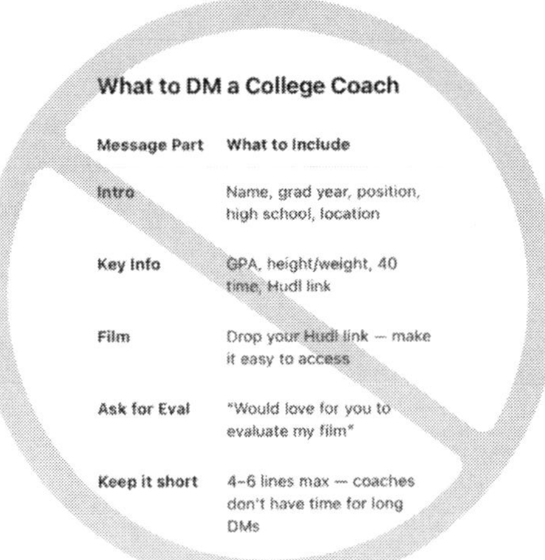

What to DM a College Coach

Message Part	What to Include
Intro	Name, grad year, position, high school, location
Key Info	GPA, height/weight, 40 time, Hudl link
Film	Drop your Hudl link — make it easy to access
Ask for Eval	"Would love for you to evaluate my film"
Keep it short	4–6 lines max — coaches don't have time for long DMs

That's why you need a simple system that's different and works every time. And that's exactly what the Perfect PITCH™ Framework is designed to do.

Each letter of the Perfect PITCH™ Framework provides your son with part of a simple, proven formula that will allow him to send a perfect recruiting message that gets a coach to actually watch your son's film and respond. This framework isn't about trying to sell a scholarship in the first message. It's about getting a foot in the door, one step at a time.

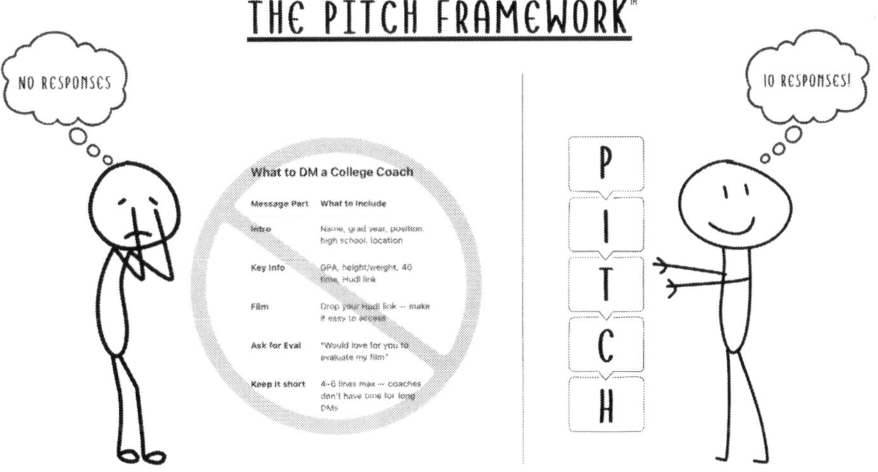

Each step is critical and has a specific purpose. Every line in your message is designed to keep the coach moving forward, just like in the area coach email. The subject line is written to get them to open the email. The referral line opens them up. The personalized line shows you did your research. The introduction gets them excited about who you are. The team fit shows them how you can specifically help them. And the call to action is there for one reason only: to get them to click the link and watch your highlight video.

But here's the real magic. As a coach reads your pitch, created using the template I am about to share with you, they are subconsciously checking off three boxes:

1. Why does this athlete want to play at our school?
2. Why does he want to play for me as the coach?
3. Why does he want to be here, on this campus, in this program?

If your message answers those three questions, the coach is far more likely to take the next step and actually invest time in watching your video.

Then, if your video has been professionally evaluated, your plays are in the right order, and you're targeting the right schools, coaches will absolutely respond, which is the final outcome you're aiming for with your message.

To be clear moving forward, I'll use the word "message" to mean either an email or a DM. You may get a response on social media or through email, but your reply should mirror the medium used to respond to you.

Before we write the pitch, it's critical that you keep your Big Board updated. Since the coach responded, we're now going to move that school on your Big Board from Coaches Contacted to Coaches Responded:

THE PERFECT PITCH™ FRAMEWORK

P = Personal Connection

The first thing your message needs is a personal connection, and the best way to do that is by mentioning the coach who referred you. This shows you've done your homework, know what you are doing, and that you're not just spamming hundreds of coaches with a copy-paste email.

Any time you can name-drop, it will help you. There is nothing more powerful than a referral, and you manufactured one in the last chapter.

- Use the name of the coach who referred you to the area coach in the subject line. We have tested many subject lines, and when you name drop who referred you, you get an extremely high open rate.
- Start the email by addressing the area coach by their last name.
- In the first sentence, mention how you found out they are the area coach by name dropping again who told you.
- Then add one personalized line showing you've done your research. Use the same personalized line process you learned from the last chapter.

Template:

Subject: (Use the word "Coach" followed by the last name of the coach who referred you)

Coach (Last Name),

(Use the word "Coach" followed by the last name of the coach who referred you) *shared with me you're the area coach for (Your City, State). (Add one personalized line.)*

Example:

Subject: *Coach Smith*

Coach Jones,

Coach Smith shared with me you're the area coach for Houston. I saw your defense just held UAB to under 200 yards. I loved watching your DBs press and fly. Congrats on only allowing 19 points per game and having 23 turnovers in 12 games.

I = Introduction

Now that you've earned their attention, introduce yourself briefly and clearly. Don't give your whole story. This should be just enough to establish who you are, what you play, where you're from, and why you are interested in their program.

Template:

My name is (Full Name), class of (class year) (position) at (your High School Name) and (why you are interested in their program).

Example:

"My name is Elijah Thomas, class of 2026 wide receiver at South Creek High in Texas and I love the air raid offense you run."

T = Team Fit with Facts

This is where most athletes go wrong. They list all their stats, but they never show how they actually fit the team. Your son needs to show the coach how he can help them win, using specific and relevant facts.

- Show how you fit the team's scheme or needs. Use coach bios to get this info.
- Use actual stats or versatility if open to other positions. And, if you don't have stats, then use intangibles.

Template:

I believe I could contribute (explain how you fit the team's scheme or needs. Use actual stats or versatility if you're open to other positions. If you don't have stats, use intangibles instead).

Example A:

"I believe I could contribute as a slot receiver in your 11 personnel. I had 1,512 receiving yards and 11 touchdowns this season."

Example B:

"Though I play quarterback, I've had D1 schools talk to me about switching to linebacker or tight end. I'm wide open to wherever you think I fit best."

- Then add why you want to be at their school specifically, beyond football. That is what can push coaches over the fence, knowing you won't just use them and leave. If you are serious about a major offered at their school, the school's location, any family ties, or a school program that appeals to you, tell them. That kind of detail shows you are not just looking for any offer. You are looking for the right one. That makes coaches more willing to invest their time in you.

Template:

I also want to be here because (insert personal reason: major, location, family connection, etc.). This isn't just a football decision for me. I believe this is the right fit on and off the field."

Example:

I also want to be here because you offer a Sports Medicine program, and that's what I want to study. This isn't just about football. I believe this is the right fit for my future too."

. . .

C = Call to Action

Remember, don't try to sell a scholarship offer. Just sell the next step. The purpose of the email is to get the coach to click the link to watch your video.

- Drop only one link. Either your Hudl, Youtube, or your player website that you created previously.
- Then ask them to book a call so they ultimately respond.

Example:

"You can see exactly what I mean by watching my highlight video here: [LINK]"

"When are you available for a quick call to discuss how I could potentially help your team?"

H = Homework and Hook

Finish strong by showing you've done extra homework and giving the coach a soft nudge to view your film or profile.

- Add a P.S. line that shows initiative.
    - Mention the completed questionnaire and feel free to also add your GPA or unique trait if it is really strong.
- Signature (Upperclassmen, after June 15 junior year)
    - *(Your First & Last Name)*
    - *(Link to Highlight Video)*
- Signature (Younger than junior year)
    - *(Your First & Last Name)*

Template:

P.S. I already completed your recruiting questionnaire (and you can also add your GPA or unique trait if it is really strong).

Example 1:

"P.S. I already completed your recruiting questionnaire."

Example 2:

"P.S. I already completed your recruiting questionnaire and I have a 4.1 GPA."

The Perfect PITCH™ Full Template:

Subject: (Use the word "Coach" followed by the last name of the coach who referred you)

Coach (Last Name),

(Use the word "Coach" followed by the last name of the coach who referred you) shared with me you're the area coach for (Your City, State). (Add one personalized line.)

My name is (Full Name), class of (class year) (position) at (your High School Name) and (why you are interested in their program).

I believe I could contribute (explain how you fit the team's scheme or needs. Use actual stats or versatility if you're open to other positions. If you don't have stats, use intangibles instead).

I also want to be here because (insert personal reason: major, location, family connection, etc.). This isn't just a football decision for me. I believe this is the right fit on and off the field."

You can see exactly what I mean by watching my highlight video here: [LINK]

When are you available for a quick call to discuss how I could potentially help your team?

P.S. I already completed your recruiting questionnaire (and you can also add your GPA or unique trait if it is really strong).

Signature (Upperclassmen, after June 15 junior year):

(Your First & Last Name)

(Link to Highlight Video)

Signature (Younger than junior year):

(Your First & Last Name)

The Perfect PITCH™ Full Template Example:

Subject: *Coach Smith*

Coach Jones,

Coach Smith shared with me you're the area coach for Houston. I saw your defense just held UAB to under 200 yards. I loved watching your DBs press and fly. Congrats on only allowing 19 points per game and having 23 turnovers in 12 games.

My name is Elijah Thomas, class of 2026 wide receiver at South Creek High in Texas and I love the air raid offense you run.

I believe I could contribute as a slot receiver in your 11 personnel. I had 1,512 receiving yards and 11 touchdowns this season.

I also want to be here because you offer a Sports Medicine program, and that's what I want to study. This isn't just about football. I believe this is the right fit for my future too."

You can see exactly what I mean by watching my highlight video here: [LINK]

When are you available for a quick call to discuss how I could potentially help your team?

P.S. I already completed your recruiting questionnaire and I have a 4.1 GPA.

Elijah Thomas

(Link to Highlight Video)

Track Your KPIs:

- Pitches Sent:
- Opened:
- Open Rate: (Goal - 50%+)
- Clicked:
- Click Rate: (Goal - 25%+)
- Replied:
- Reply Rate: (Goal - 18%+)

	PITCHES SENT	OPENED	OPEN %	CLICKED	CLICK %	REPLIED	REPLY %
	10	6	60%	3	30%	2	20%
	10	7	70%	4	40%	2	20%
	10	5	50%	1	10%	0	0%

Use the KPIs above as your benchmark for success. If you're sending messages but not getting replies, track your KPIs and adjust:

- Low Open Rate = You aren't using the right subject line.
- Low Click Rate = Your pitch is not sufficient and you need to improve your pitch.
- Low Response Rate = Messaging coaches at the wrong level of play or your highlight video is still not optimized. Get an unbiased professional evaluation from a recent college football coach or recruiting director. If you want our team, who has these credentials, to do it, visit GoNextPlay.com/Evaluation)

Now, that you've sent your pitch, you will move the school from the Coaches Responded stage to the Area Coach ID stage:

WHEN A COACH REACHES OUT TO YOU FIRST: 5-STEP RESPONSE SYSTEM

Step 1: Always Respond Immediately

- Be prompt. This shows you're serious.
- Even if you're not interested in the school, always reply. The college football world is small and coaches talk. Plus, they might move to a school you would go to and now you have the relationship.

Step 2: Respond with a Phone Call and Voicemail

- If they included their number either intentionally or it is in their signature, call them right away. If they don't answer, leave a voicemail. This is another reason it is important to have your son do the outreach so he can call them immediately.

Voicemail example:

"Hey Coach (last Name), this is (Your Name). I just received your message and I look forward to speaking. Give me a call back at (Your Number) when you can."

Step 3: Respond with a Video Message and End with a Question

- The coach may share with you where they are in the Offer Funnel™. If they do, choose the question below that matches their stage in the funnel. If you're unsure, default to the highlight video question. Ending with a question keeps the conversation going and gives the coach a clear next step.
- Then respond on the platform that they originally reached out to you on.
- Just like your son did during the area coach outreach, if a coach reaches out on social media, he should respond with the same message, but as a video message.

Template:

Coach (Last Name),

I just left you a quick voicemail. Thanks again for reaching out. (Personalized Line, ie. I saw your defense held (Opponent) to under 14 points last week. Impressive.)

I'd love to connect and talk more. Have you had a chance to watch my highlight video yet?

(Link to video)

Looking forward to hearing from you.

(Your First & Last Name)

Here are additional questions your son can ask, depending on where the coach is in the Offer Funnel™:

- *"Have you had a chance to watch my highlight video?"*
- *"When would be a good time to jump on a quick call?"*
- *"When would be a good time to visit campus?"*
- *"What do I need to do to earn an offer?"*

Step 4: Follow-Up

- After you send the message, add the school to your big board.
- Then create a task to follow up if you don't hear back in seven days.
- Make sure to follow-up in the same thread 3-5 times.
- Call again the next day as well. Be persistent.

Step 5: Use Leverage to Create Urgency

- If one coach in a conference reaches out, let the other coaches in the same division know. Typically, if one school is interested, others will be too. This is a great opportunity to create momentum and expand your options.
- Add these schools that you are interested in to your Big Board, and begin the Area Coach process for each. Just make a slight tweak to your personalized line, as shown in the example below.

Email Template:

School: *(School Name)*

Coach (Last Name),

Coach Sanders at Idaho State recently reached out to me, and so I started doing research on your program. I really like what I'm seeing in (School Name), especially (Personalized Line).

Who would be the area coach responsible for [City, State]?

Looking forward to hearing back,

(Your Name)

By sending it this way, you are creating FOMO (fear of missing out), and coaches are more likely to respond.

Now, after everything you've learned in this chapter, you can't expect your son to write the perfect pitch on the first try. Perfecting a pitch takes time, repetition, and small adjustments based on actual feedback from college coaches.

Consistency builds momentum, leading to more video views, more responses, and more offers. Just like you wouldn't step onto the field without practicing the plays, you shouldn't send a pitch without refining it, over and over again.

For the athletes I mentor, we typically go through five or six versions before we finalize their initial pitch. And that pitch keeps evolving as they evolve, not just as football players, but as young men learning how to market themselves, speak with confidence, and create real opportunities.

As they grow, so does their story. That means new film, better stats, new offers, and more belief in what they bring to the table. It's a living message. Always improving.

And when you do it right, and use your KPIs to identify and improve where you're struggling, it flat-out works, even in the most unlikely situations.

THE RIGHT PITCH CHANGES EVERYTHING

I remember having to rework Kegan Setliff's pitch many times over. He didn't play for a big-name school. In fact, his entire graduating class had just 10 students. He played 6-man football in a tiny Texas town at a school no college coach had ever heard of. Plus, he was only 5'9". On paper, he didn't stand a chance.

But Kegan had heart. He had the talent, but he needed the right pitch. So we built it from scratch. We highlighted his speed, toughness, and versatility in a way that made coaches stop scrolling, click, and watch. And when he tore his MCL during the season, right when most players would've disappeared from a coach's radar, we didn't back down. We rewrote the pitch again.

Each version of Kegan's pitch was really a new chapter in his story. As his situation changed, we updated the way he told it. That's what kept coaches engaged.

Four different versions of his pitch in just one season. And it worked. Kegan didn't just get noticed and he didn't just get multiple scholarship offers. He became the first football player in his school's history to sign a Division II scholarship.

Kegan Setliff's Family & Richie Contartesi at Signing Day

That's the power of getting your pitch right, even when the odds are stacked against you.

KEY TAKEAWAYS

- Sell the next step, don't aim directly for the scholarship. Focus your pitch on one thing —getting the coach to watch your film.
- No one can sell your son better than he can. Not the parents, a trainer, or a recruiting service. It has to come from him.

- Your son will face rejection. It hurts more when it's personal, but learning to handle it now will give him a huge edge for life.
- The Perfect PITCH™ Framework is powerful when used correctly. Every line in your message has a purpose, to keep the coach moving forward.
- The athletes who get the most traction are the ones who personalize their pitch, both in how they fit the team and why they want to be at that school beyond football.
- Your pitch is never final. Your son must master storytelling. The pitch is not just a message, it's his story. And the athletes who know how to tell their evolving story are the ones who get remembered, build trust, and win offers.
- Tracking KPIs matters. Use your data to make adjustments and improve your pitch, don't just guess if you aren't successful.
- Whenever you are stuck, always reference back to The Offer Funnel™.

YOUR NEXT PLAY

- Help your son build his Perfect PITCH™. Walk him through each letter of the framework step by step so nothing gets missed.
- Have him write his first version. Don't expect it to be perfect. He should plan to revise it three to five times before it's ready.
- Track his KPIs. Use the tracking sheet to monitor opens, clicks, and replies. This data will show where he needs to improve.
- Update his Big Board. If a coach responds or shares who the area coach is, update that school's status right away.
- Make sure he starts replying to coaches as soon as possible. Encourage him to take action.
- Prepare him for rejection. Remind him that rejection is normal. It's not personal, it's part of the process, and it's how he gets better.
- Keep evolving his message. As he improves, his pitch should too. Better film, stronger stats, more offers, and more confidence should all show up in his message.

PLAY 10: SECURE VISITS

"Selling is not telling. Selling is asking the right questions and letting the prospect convince themselves."

TOM HOPKINS

My phone rang on a Thursday night. It was the mom of a junior offensive lineman from North Carolina. Her voice cracked right away.

"Coach Richie...we're stuck. My son is getting a lot of interest, but nothing's happening."

Their son had the film and grades. A few FCS and D2 schools had even messaged him back. But it always stopped there. No visits. No offers. Not even a phone call.

She said, "I don't get it. He gets messages, coaches say they're interested, but then it goes quiet. He's not getting on the phone with anyone. I've told him over and over to follow up, to try and get them on a call, but he just keeps waiting. He says they'll come to him, and now it feels like it's slipping away."

So I jumped on a Zoom with her son the next day. He sat there in a hoodie, camera barely showing his face. He looked frustrated, but mostly defeated.

I asked, "Tell me what happens after a coach replies." He shrugged. "I say thanks. And then I wait."

"And do they ever get back to you?" He shook his head.

That's where he was stuck, right between interest and action. The coach had replied, but the athlete didn't know how to take the coach through the sales process yet. He didn't know how to lead.

I told him straight up, "You don't get recruited by waiting. They're evaluating another 70,000 players and can't remember everyone. You have to get the coach on the phone, sell yourself, and then sell the visit."

He leaned in, confused. "Sell it how?"

"By asking the right questions. When you ask good questions, coaches talk more. And when they talk more, they start to like you. Plus, they know you're serious and being recruited by other schools, which creates more demand. That's how you go from 'We're interested' to 'Let's bring you in for a visit.'"

He asked, "How do you know that?"

I knew that because I had to learn the hard way myself. When I first started in business, I used to get people on sales calls and completely freeze. I'd talk and talk, trying to explain everything we did. But people didn't buy.

Then one day, my mentor told me something I'll never forget, he quoted Tom Hopkins, "Selling is not telling. Selling is asking the right questions and letting the prospect convince themselves."

Then he shared with me what questions to ask and how to ask them. That changed the game for me. I started asking instead of pitching.

"What are you struggling with?"

"What made you book this call?"

"What do you need help with most?"

And you know what happened? People opened up. They told me exactly what they needed. And then if it made sense to continue the process, they asked me how to get started.

And because I'm so systems oriented and I forget things easily, I had to build a system that showed me exactly what to say next, no matter which direction the conversation went. That's when my mentor and I created what I now teach every athlete I mentor, the WIN Framework™.

W = Want – What does the coach want at your position?

I = Issue – What challenge is the coach trying to solve?

N = Next Play – What is the next play?

I've used this exact framework in my business and sales, and now this framework is helping athletes turn interest into visits, and visits into offers.

Because asking questions is the real secret. Not just to recruiting, but to sales, trust, and leadership. So that's exactly what I taught him next.

We went to work. We role-played the entire call, just like it was game day. I coached him on everything, take the hoodie off your head, sit up straight, smile, speak clearly, and look at the camera, not off to the side.

I told him, "The way you present yourself on a call matters just as much as what you say." We practiced tone, posture, and pacing. Every detail. Because that's what coaches are looking for too. They're not purposely looking for it, but they can feel confidence, and confidence pushes coaches to the next step of the sales process.

We kept practicing. Over and over. I taught him how to ask what the coach was looking for in a lineman, what challenges they were facing at that position, and how he could help solve those problems. Then we worked on how to ask, confidently, "Coach, what are the next steps? I've got my calendar up. Are there a few dates that work for a visit?"

That was the play. A week later, he got on a call with one of the D2 coaches who'd ghosted him. And for the first time, he didn't just thank the coach for responding and hang up. He led.

He asked the questions. He guided the conversation. He sold the visit. Two days later, that same coach booked him for an official visit. A month after that, they offered him a scholarship.

Wow. If one coaching session could make that big of a difference for him, how many other athletes are missing out just because no one ever coached them on how to communicate confidently with college coaches? They wouldn't listen to Mom and Dad because, well, they're just "Mom and Dad."

That's when I realized how critical and powerful that coaching session was. Today, we've made that session part of our application process.

After a family applies to work with us, the first step is for our team, with over 25 years of Division I recruiting experience, to do a full professional evaluation of his game film. We determine his current level (D1-P5, D1-G5, D1-FCS, D2, D3, or NAIA), reorder game clips so coaches actually keep watching his highlight reel, and most importantly, provide clear feedback on exactly what he needs to improve to reach the next level.

Then we do an athlete interview to make sure he meets our criteria and coach him on his communication and interviewing skills. Parents are always shocked at how we coach their sons up during our interview process, even before we decide to work together.

We teach athletes how to communicate like pros so they're prepared when they get in front of a college coach, whether we work together or not. Because interviews are part of recruiting now, and most kids just aren't ready.

But this player showed up. And he learned fast. That one conversation changed everything.

And the truth is, I only knew how to teach him that because I missed opportunities when I went through the recruiting process and had to learn it in business the hard way first. That one offensive lineman's story started the same way so many do—interest, but no action.

Yet once he learned how to ask the right questions, everything changed. That one shift turned interest into action, and it led to a visit, then a scholarship.

THE WIN FRAMEWORK™

Congratulations. Your son identified the area coach, sent his pitch, the coach watched his highlight video and responded with interest. This is the part of The Offer Funnel™ where it's all about one thing. Getting that coach on a phone call so your son can sell him on a visit.

Remember, we are only selling the next step. That next step is getting on a phone call, and then during that call, selling the visit. We are not trying to sell an offer right now. This call is about building a relationship, building trust, getting the coach to like your son, and moving them forward in the sales process. One step at a time.

Most athletes think if they can just explain their story, their stats, and how bad they want it, the coach will offer them. But coaches don't care how bad you want it until they believe you can help their team. And they won't believe that unless you understand their world.

Asking great questions changes everything. It shows maturity. It shows preparation. It shows your son is serious. And it gives him a clear path to the next step. If you want a visit, stop trying to pitch it and start asking your way there.

The WIN Framework™ is the 3-step system your son will use in every phone call, in-person conversation, or back-and-forth message with a coach. It works in every interaction, even when the coach takes the conversation in a new direction.

Why? Because no two conversations are exactly the same. That's why you can't follow a word-for-word script. Instead, this framework gives your son a clear map so he never gets lost or stuck. It keeps him in control, and it helps him keep moving the coach through the recruiting process. Here's how it works, in more detail:

W = Want

What does the coach want in a player for your son's position?

I = Issue

What challenges is the coach trying to solve on the team right now?

N = Next Play

What is the next step in the recruiting process, and how do we schedule it right now?

These are the three questions your son needs to answer by the end of the call or conversation. There are lots of different questions your son will ask throughout the conversation. But if he can always get these answers, he'll be in control of the conversation and moving the coach toward a visit.

Every conversation is going to sound a little different. And that's okay. What matters is that your son knows what he's listening for. For example, let's say your son asks:

"Coach, what are you looking for in a wide receiver?"

The coach might say:

"We need guys who can block, run clean routes, and aren't afraid to take a hit across the middle."

Now, your son doesn't just move on. He asks:

"What does that look like in your offense?"

The coach explains. Then your son can share a sentence or two on how he can possibly help that coach. He may say:

"Over the last 4 years, I was the go-to pass catcher over the middle. Not only taking big hits, but also breaking some of those tackles and taking it to the house."

Your son then asks a follow-up. They go back and forth for a bit. That's a good thing. Because at the end of that back-and-forth, your son knows exactly what that coach wants.

Same thing with the Issue. It might take a few questions to figure out what challenge the coach is trying to solve. Maybe the depth chart is thin. Maybe they don't have a consistent third-down option. But as long as your son keeps asking good questions and listening, he'll find the answer.

And that's the whole point of the WIN Framework™. It keeps your son in control. It makes sure he doesn't waste the conversation. It helps him build trust, and it gives him the information he needs to share with the coach exactly how he can help that program and move the coach to the Next Play.

Other players will just pitch coaches without having any idea what that coach actually wants or what challenges that coach is facing. That's annoying. You don't like being pitched that way either, right? Instead, we only share how we can help, if we actually can help and it's a good fit. Coaches will love you for it.

This is how your son sells a visit the right way. He doesn't pitch until he knows what the coach wants. He does it by asking smart questions, listening, and leading the conversation. Every great athlete asks, listens, and leads with confidence. That is what the WIN Framework™ is built to do.

Let's walk through exactly how your son can book and lead a call with a coach, and ultimately turn that call into a visit.

Step 1: Set the Call

If a coach responds to a message, reply with this template:

Coach [Last Name],

Thanks for the response. I'm really looking forward to speaking with you. Can you share a few times that you're available for a quick call and I will make one work?

*Or feel free to use this link to book a time that works best: [Insert Calendar Link]***

Looking forward to it,

[Your Name]

**I create a booking calendar for the players I mentor because it makes it easy for the coach to pick and schedule a time that works for them. The calendar sends reminders by email and text which helps make sure the coach shows up. Coaches get busy and sometimes forget. You can use the calendar inside the Next Play CRM or set one up using a tool like Calendly.com. Just make sure it is simple and fast for the coach to book a time.

If the coach sends their number, call immediately. If they don't answer, leave this voicemail:

"Hey Coach [Last Name], this is [Your Name]. I just got your message and look forward to speaking. You can call or text me at [Your Number]. Let me know a good time to call."

Make sure to update your big board after you book the call:

Interested Schools	Questionnaire Complete	Coaches Contacted	Coaches Responded	Area Coach ID	Calls Booked	Visit	Scholarship Offer
					Ole Miss		

Step 2: Prepare for the Call

Help your son get set up with this checklist:

Technical Setup

- Phone fully charged
- Strong cell or Wi-Fi signal
- Quiet place with no distractions
- If it's a Zoom or video call, test the video software before the meeting. Make sure it works and check if you need to download anything ahead of time. You do not want to be late.
- Have a backup way to contact the coach if needed

Materials

- Highlight film link ready to send or reference
- Have your transcripts ready to send with one click
- Pen and paper for notes
- Calendar link open and ready to schedule a visit

Mentality

- Research done on the school, program, and coach
- Practice done with your mentor or parent using the WIN Framework
- Calm, focused, confident, and ready to learn—not pitch.

Be ready to answer these commonly asked questions from coaches:

- What's your GPA and test scores?
- What do you want to study in college?
- What are your strengths and weaknesses as a player?
- What's your training routine like?
- Why do you want to play at this school?
- Are other schools recruiting you right now?
- What makes you believe you can compete at this level?

Like I've said many times in this playbook, the more you practice, the better you'll be. You would never go into a game without running the plays first. It's the same on the business side. Make sure you role-play with your mentor or parents at least 15-20 times before your first call. This one call could save you $2,500 by turning an unofficial visit into an official one. Or it could earn you a $200,000 scholarship. Never leave anything up to chance.

Assignment:

- Print out all the commonly asked questions at GoNextPlay.com/resources, write down your answers, and have your son role-play with you or his mentor.

Step 3: Start the Call With Confidence

Open the conversation with this script:

"Coach, thanks for taking the time to speak with me. I did some research on your [offense, defense, or special teams] and I love how you [insert something specific]. I think my skill set MAY be able to help the team, but you know way more than me about the team so I'm really looking forward to learning about you, the team, and your program to see if there is a good fit."

Then immediately lead into your first question to stay in control of the conversation:

So I am curious, what qualities do you look for in a (your position)?

Step 4: Use the WIN Framework™ to Lead the Conversation

Although the conversation should feel natural and not like a formal interview, these are the core questions that guide every conversation. They help your son take control, show leadership, and sell a visit by asking, not pitching.

As always, make sure your son role-plays this with his mentor or parents at least 15-20 times before the first call.

W = Want

- *What qualities do you look for in a (your position)?*
- *What type of player succeeds in your system?*

I = Issue

- *What challenges are you facing at (your position) this year?*
- *How can a player like me help the team?*

N = Next Play (There will always be interchangeable questions throughout the conversation, but these are the mandatory questions your son must ask at the end of the call.)

- *What are the next steps in the recruiting process?*
- *Is there an opportunity to visit the campus and meet some of the team members?*
- *Would it be an official or unofficial visit?*
- *I have my calendar up now, what are a few dates that work on your end?*

This last question is responsible for more booked visits and fewer follow-ups than anything else. Most players get excited in the moment and forget to ask. They tell themselves they'll book the visit later. But sometimes, getting back in touch with that coach is nearly impossible. Don't wait. Get it scheduled on the call.

These questions above must be answered, but if the conversation is flowing, your son can keep it going with other optional questions you may have. Here are a few suggestions to help or spark ideas for your own:

Football-Related Questions:

- What's the coaching philosophy here, both on and off the field?
- How does redshirting work in your program, and under what circumstances might a player be redshirted?
- How would you evaluate the current depth chart for my position?
- What's the off-season training program like?
- Are there opportunities for players to take on leadership roles within the team?
- How do you assist players in balancing athletics with academics?

Academic Questions:

- What academic support systems are in place for student-athletes?

- How flexible is the football schedule in accommodating major-specific classes or labs?
- Are there any academic achievement awards or recognitions within the sports department?

Team Culture & Campus Life:

- How would you describe the team culture here?
- What's a typical day or week like for a player during the season and off-season?

Personal Interest:

- I've always admired [specific player or strategy of the team]. Can you tell me more about how that developed?
- What would you say are the biggest challenges and rewards of playing for this program?
- How do players typically spend their free time or off-days during the season?
- How do you help prepare players who are aiming for a professional football career?

Reminder: You lead a call by asking questions based on the coach's responses. Do not ask a question, ignore the answer, then move to a completely different question. Make it a conversation.

Step 5: Schedule the Visit

If the coach is interested and says "yes", your son should book the visit on the call. Confirm:

- Date
- Time
- Location
- Who your son will be meeting with and who to ask for when you get there.
- Also discuss accommodations including hotel, airfare, and car or ride pickup if it's an official visit.

If the coach hesitates to confirm a visit, say this to ensure you still move forward in the process:

"Totally understand. Would it help to schedule a quick follow-up call next week? That way we both stay on the same page."

Then book the call using your custom calendar so it sends the calendar invite and reminders automatically.

Here are the different types of visits to be prepared to discuss and potentially ask for. It will depend on where you are in the recruiting process.

Junior Day (Unofficial)

- Paid for by the family
- Usually group settings for underclassmen
- Great for early exposure
- Focus on being present and engaged

Camps (Unofficial)

- Paid for by the family
- Great for building relationships
- Validates physical play and attributes

Game Day Visit (Can be Official or Unofficial)

- Can be paid for by the family or the program
- Focused on seeing the atmosphere
- Great opportunity to engage and visualize being on the team

Official Visit

- Paid for by the program
- 48 hours of high-level attention and structure
- Includes deep conversations, meals, dorms, game day, and more
- Only one per school (but unlimited schools)

Make sure to update your big board after your visit is scheduled:

Interested Schools	Questionnaire Complete	Coaches Contacted	Coaches Responded	Area Coach ID	Calls Booked	Visit	Scholarship Offer
						Ole Miss	

Step 6: Follow Up

If the coach says they'll get back to you with more info or dates for a visit but doesn't, your son should absolutely stay persistent. The coach was interested enough to get on a call, so don't give up. You might need to improve how you sell the visit, or the coach just isn't ready yet. The key word is *yet*.

Sales is a skill, and it takes time to get good at. Your son will improve with every call. His conversion rate from phone call to scheduled visit will get better over time as long as he keeps role-playing, reviewing his calls, and getting more attempts.

So send this message in the same communication thread you were using before the call:

"Hey (Coach Last Name), It was great speaking. I'm still very interested and would love the opportunity to visit your campus. Were you able to find a few available dates?"

Coaches are busy, so following up is mandatory—and keeps your son on the coach's radar. This is also why posting on social media daily is critical to staying top of mind. Make a task to follow up every week for the next 3-5 weeks.

Also, make sure your son treats these calls like game film. After each one, replay it in his mind or review any notes. Ask: What went well? What could he have done better? What should he do next time?

Just like reviewing football film, this is how he gets better at sales. That loop of call, reflect, adjust, and role-play is how he becomes a pro at selling visits.

Step 7: Send a Thank-You Note

Right after the call, have your son send a short thank-you message in the same conversation thread. Then, write and mail a physical thank-you note. Almost no recruits do this. It makes a big difference.

Final Follow-Up Message (if coach has not scheduled the visit yet):

"Hey Coach [Last Name], it was great speaking. I'm still very interested and would love the opportunity to visit your campus. Were you able to find a few available dates?"

Thank-You Message (after coach books the visit):

"Hey Coach [Last Name], thank you again for taking the time to speak with me. I'm really looking forward to the visit and appreciate the opportunity. See you soon."

I highly recommend adding something personal from the call to the thank-you note. This shows your son was paying attention and that he truly cares.

Bonus Tip: Keep the coach updated with new achievements. This helps your son stay top of mind. Here are a few great reasons to follow up:

- New film
- Awards or recognition
- New stats or accomplishments

Always close with: "Would now be a good time to schedule that visit?"

That one question changed everything for Cruz Castellanos.

THE CRITICAL QUESTION

Most coaches saw an undersized lineman and moved on. It's the one position on the football field that is almost impossible to get a scholarship if you don't have the size, but Cruz refused to be overlooked.

He followed this exact playbook with relentless consistency. One school showed interest after watching his film. But the coach didn't schedule anything. Just said, "We'll be in touch."

That's the point most players give up. Not Cruz.

He followed up. He sent a thank-you note. He sent a new clip of him pancaking a guy twice his size. And then, finally the coach scheduled a call with him.

On the call, he asked the right questions throughout the call which led to a natural close.

"Coach, I'd love the chance to visit and meet the team. Is there an opportunity to visit the campus and meet some of the team members?

Would it be an official or unofficial visit?

I have my calendar up now, what are a few dates that work on your end?"

That call made the difference.

The coach booked the official visit. Cruz followed the rest of this playbook and two weeks later, he got the call every athlete dreams of, *"We'd like to offer you a scholarship."*

Cruz didn't beg. He didn't hope. He sold himself by leading conversations the right way, with questions. That's how he moved a coach through The Offer Funnel™, one step at a time.

And that's exactly how your son can, too.

KEY TAKEAWAYS

- Selling is not telling, it's asking the right questions.
- The WIN Framework™ (Want, Issue, Next Play) helps your son lead every conversation.
- Conversations create conversions. A phone call gives your son the best shot at earning an official visit.
- Great players don't wing it. They prepare, practice, and execute, just like in a game.
- The goal isn't to sell a scholarship. The goal is to sell the next step, the visit.
- Every great recruiting call ends with a scheduled visit or a clear follow-up plan.
- Confidence is coachable. Even if your son struggles on calls now, this is a skill he can master.

YOUR NEXT PLAY

- Create a calendar link (using tools like Calendly.com or Next Play CRM) to make it easy for coaches to book calls with your son
- Choose five smart questions from the WIN Framework™ that your son will ask on every call
- Print out and complete the Commonly Asked Questions coaches may ask, and write down your son's answers
- Role-play those answers as well as the entire call with your son at least 15 times before he gets on the phone with a coach
- Prepare a quiet space and check tech before every call—audio, lighting, and camera presence matter
- Book the visit on the call using the final question: "I have my calendar up now, what are a few dates that work on your end?"
- Send a thank-you message and a handwritten note immediately after every call
- Update the Big Board to track call results and visit status
- Set a weekly follow-up reminder for any coach who hasn't booked the visit yet
- Keep coaches updated with new achievements (film, awards, stats) and always close with, "Would now be a good time to schedule that visit?"

I'd Love To Hear From You

Thank you so much for reading this book-it means the world to me. If you found it helpful, inspiring, or just enjoyable, would you take a moment to leave a review?

Your feedback not only helps others but also keeps me motivated to create more valuable content for you.

Here's how you can leave a review:

1. Scan the QR code on this page to go directly to the review page.
2. Or, visit your Amazon Orders page, find this book, and click "Write a Product Review."

Your kind words make a big difference. Thank you for your support!

4TH QUARTER: GENERATE OFFERS

PLAY 11: ASK FOR THE OFFER

"If you don't ask, the answer is always no."

JIM ROHN

It was a Thursday afternoon at Ole Miss, and as soon as the final whistle blew at practice, I took off running. My legs were heavy, but I didn't stroll. I sprinted through the field gate, down the tunnel, and into the locker room hallway.

Every Thursday, the coaches posted the travel squad list just outside the locker room door. That one piece of paper decided who got to suit up on Saturday and who didn't. If your name wasn't on it, you weren't traveling. You weren't dressing. You weren't playing.

And every Thursday, I was the first one there. I'd run straight to the wall, shoulder pads still on, dripping sweat, eyes locked on that list, praying today might be different. But week after week, it wasn't. And every week, for three straight years, my name wasn't there.

I can't explain how much that hurts. It's hard to understand unless you've lived it. Unless you've worked every day, done everything right, and still come up short over and over again. There were nights I questioned if I belonged. Days I wondered if the coaches would ever believe in me.

I had been so hungry just to get in the door. But after I'd kicked that door open, I realized how far away I still was. It was just the beginning. Staying on the team, solidifying a role, and earning a scholarship in the SEC was a whole different level.

Three years of scout-team reps. Three years of early morning lifts, late-night film sessions, and brutal practices. Getting picked up and slammed to the ground daily during the Oklahoma drill by linebackers who weighed 100 pounds more than me.

No game days, no rewards, and no bright lights. The excitement of simply "being on the team" was finally starting to wear off. Just more bruises, more silence, and the quiet disappointment of walking past the travel squad list with my name missing, again.

Most people today can't wait three days for results, let alone three months. I waited three years. And finally, after I'd had enough, I called my dad.

"Dad, I don't think this is going to work. I've given everything. And I still haven't played a single down. This is a waste of time and makes no sense to continue."

He didn't say anything right away. "I know what you're going to say," I told him. "You have a choice, you can quit like everyone else, or you keep going and focus on your next play."

There was a long pause. Then his voice softened. "Richie…you don't have anything left to prove." But that statement cut the deepest, because I wanted to prove to myself I could do it.

Since the day I did not pass 5th grade, I'd felt like a failure. And deep down, I craved finally making my parents proud. I needed it like a drowning man needs air. I had to show them I could do it.

I wanted this to be the thing that finally made them proud. And I didn't want to come up short, not again. So I hung up the phone, wiped my face, and got back to work.

That final summer before my senior year, I was the only one in the weight room trying to get stronger every single day. I was the only one in the film room trying to get smarter every single day. I was the only one out on the field, working on my craft, running routes alone every single day.

And I did all of it while wanting to quit. Every. Single. Day. But I didn't quit, because I refused to let this story end without actually playing, earning a scholarship, and contributing in games.

That's when a spot opened up. Not on offense. Not on defense. But on special teams.

People asked me, "So you must've been the kickoff returner, right?"

Nope.

"Punt returner?"

Nope.

"Oh, then you were the guy who ran down the field and made the big hit, right?"

Nope.

The special teams coordinator had seen me all summer, in the film room, in the weight room, and on the field every single day.

One afternoon, while I was out catching passes in the indoor practice facility, he walked in and said, "Richie, I've watched you for three years, and I don't think I've ever seen you drop a pass.

I need a field goal holder I can trust, someone who's going to catch every snap and be exactly where I need them to be, when I need them to be there. Start working with the kickers, because I'm going to make you the new field goal holder."

I said, "Yes sir, Coach," calmly, waiting for him to leave the facility. Then, once the door shut behind him, I jumped in the air and shouted, "Yes!"

Yeah, I know. You might be laughing right now. And that's okay. But that's because most people don't understand how a college football roster works.

Being named the field goal holder guaranteed me a spot on the travel squad list. That meant I'd be dressed for every game. And with only a limited number of players making the trip, it meant my receivers coach would finally have access to play me.

I wasn't just another walk-on stuck on the practice squad, buried on the depth chart. I was in the room. For the first time, I had a real shot to earn a spot at receiver. To prove I belonged. Without being on that travel list, you don't have a chance.

Now, I knew playing on the field goal team wasn't going to earn me a scholarship. Yet, over the summer I had slowly but surely been climbing the wide receiver depth chart.

When I first made the team, I wasn't even on it. As the years went on, I moved from off the depth chart to on it at fifteenth, then to twelfth, to ninth, and finally to seventh. But to actually be in the rotation, you had to be in the top six. By training camp, I knew I was going to get there.

And now that I had a spot on special teams, I finally had a real shot at playing receiver. For the first time, I had the confidence to do something no other walk-on would even think about.

Ask.

ASK

My dad always used to say, "Ask, and you shall receive." Well, I had contributed to the team for three years. I earned a role on special teams. I was moving up the receiver depth chart and about to be in the starting rotation. Plus, since I was a senior, this was my last shot.

So I went up the stairs to the head coach's office, palms sweating, and heart racing. I walked in, looked him in the eye, and said, "Coach, I love this program and I want to keep finding ways to contribute at the highest level possible. What do I need to do to earn a scholarship?"

To my surprise, he said, "Richie, this was already on my mind and I'm open to it." Then he gave me a few things to work on. I said, "Yes sir, Coach," and got to work.

When I finished, I came back and told him I'd done what he asked. Then he gave me more. This went on for a few weeks. No offer yet, but I wasn't letting up.

Training camp started. And even though I was locked in on that scholarship, I still didn't have it. But that didn't matter. I knew the only way forward was the same as it had always been—earn it.

So I kept showing up. I kept making plays. I kept proving myself, again and again. Finally, I worked my way up to number six on the depth chart.

Ole Miss Football Depth Chart

We had one final scrimmage right before the season started. I walked into the locker room, took a deep breath, and started to get dressed for what was the most pivotal and meaningful scrimmage of my life. One last shot to prove myself.

I was locked in and laser focused. I put on my pads and helmet and began walking through the tunnel into the stadium. There was a bright blue sky, fans in the stands, and I could smell the muggy grass.

As I walked through the tunnel, I took one final deep breath and remembered to just stay focused on my next play. One play at a time. I began warming up and had started sweating when I felt a tap on my shoulder. I turned around and it was the head coach, Houston Nutt.

He looked me in the eyes. And for a second, everything slowed down. All I could think about were the people who said I couldn't do it. I thought about all my friends who told me going to Oxford, Mississippi was a waste of time. I thought about all the rejection, like the meeting at FIU where the coach never showed up, or the coach at JU who cut me before I even had a chance.

I thought about the teacher who pulled me out into the hallway after I failed fifth grade and told me I wouldn't be worth anything. I thought about every time someone told me I wasn't big enough. Wasn't fast enough. Wasn't talented enough.

But on this day, in Vaught-Hemingway Stadium, standing face to face with the head football coach at Ole Miss, Coach Nutt looked me in the eyes and said, "Richie...you've earned it. You're now on scholarship, congratulations."

I didn't say a word. I couldn't. 15 years of scraping, clawing, and suffering, all for this one dream. Every early morning. Every injury. Every coach who said I wasn't big enough. Every friend who said I didn't have a chance.

It all flashed through my mind like a movie. And in that moment, I wasn't thinking about myself. I was thinking about my dad. I was thinking about my mom. I was thinking about the young boy who printed out the University of Miami scholarship requirements, signed it, and taped it to his wall.

I just stared back at Coach Nutt, held back tears, and said, "I won't let you down, Coach." After the scrimmage, I sprinted to the locker room. Threw on my clothes. Grabbed my phone. Ran straight to my truck.

I called my mom first. She was so excited and literally screamed. Then I called my dad. The phone rang once, twice, three times.

And finally, he answered. "Hey Richie, what's up?" I was quiet for a second. Then I said, "Dad...it just happened." He said, "What?"

"I did it. I just got put on scholarship." He didn't say anything. Just silence. Then he took a breath... and said the words I'd been chasing since I was in 5th grade.

"I'm proud of you."

I lost it. I sat in my truck, head on the steering wheel, tears pouring out of me. Because in that one moment, every practice, every rejection, every Thursday travel list I was never on with no reward, suddenly made sense. I wasn't just doing it to prove myself right.

I was also doing it to make my parents proud. And for every parent who ever sacrificed so their kid could have a shot. For every dad who coached from the sideline. For every mom who sat in the stands with her heart in her throat. For every son who just wanted to hear, "I'm proud of you."

But that kind of moment doesn't just happen. I didn't wait for the scholarship to fall into my lap. It had to be earned. And when the time comes, you don't wait, you ask. Not for the outcome. Not for the scholarship. You ask what needs to be done to earn it.

I had already proven my value, but the coaches needed to know how badly I wanted it.

I'd still be on the sideline if I hadn't…stuck with it when I wanted to quit, earned a roster spot by fighting my way up the receiver depth chart, found ways to make the team better, and, finally, asked how to earn it.

Yet I didn't do it alone. I had a mentor who guided me through every one of those moments, who challenged me, believed in me, and showed me what it really meant to earn it. Most importantly, he gave me confidence. Without him, I wouldn't have made it.

And your son won't either. Not if he doesn't learn how to ask at the right time, in the right way. This chapter is about how to do exactly that. Because your son isn't just fighting for a scholarship. He's fighting for that moment. The one that makes everything worth it.

It's how to ask the right way, at the right time. And this applies whether you're in high school, in college, or in any life situation where you've earned something but just haven't received it yet. Like the raise you deserve at work. Or the girl of your dreams.

I'm not talking about asking for handouts. I'm talking about stepping up and having the courage to ask for what you've earned. Because at the end of the day, it's the squeaky wheel that gets the offer.

And if your son is going to experience his moment, if he's going to hang up the phone one day and say, "Coach just offered me a scholarship," then he has to learn this critical skill.

Because in every interaction with a coach, a sale is taking place. Either your son is selling the coach on why he deserves a scholarship, or the coach is selling your son on why he doesn't. Either way, a sale takes place.

One of them walks away convinced. That's the game.

But don't worry. Your son doesn't have to be a smooth talker. He doesn't have to be loud or extroverted. He doesn't even have to *like* sales. Because the truth is, he's been doing it his whole life.

Think about it. Babies sell their parents on why they should be fed, rocked, held. And they win, every time. A toddler sells you on why he should get five more minutes before bedtime.

Your son sold his first crush on why she should say yes to being his girlfriend. He sold his friends on what movie to watch or what restaurant to go to.

We are always selling.

Every time you ask someone for something you want, and you care how they respond, you're selling. You're presenting a case for why they should agree.

The problem is, as people get older and face more and more rejection, they start pulling back. They stop asking. Not because they don't want something, but because they're afraid to feel the pain of hearing "no."

And it makes sense. We're wired as humans to avoid pain at all costs. Physical pain. Emotional pain. Social pain. That sting of rejection, even just the thought of it, is often enough to stop people from even trying.

It's one of the biggest reasons people settle for average. In their jobs. In business. In relationships.

Instead of stepping up to the plate and creating a life of abundance, they shrink back. They choose safety over significance. Comfort over calling.

But if your son wants the offer, he has to lean into the moment most people avoid. Not because he loves selling. But because he loves the game. He loves the dream.

And he's willing to do what others won't to get it. Why? Because he knows there's no failure, only his Next Play™.

That's why this chapter exists. Because it's not about being salesy. It's about being ready, prepared, and confident. And it all starts with understanding what "closing" really is.

When most people hear the word "sales," they picture the wrong thing. They think of the pushy used car salesman. The fake smile. The pressure tactics.

Someone trying to convince you to buy something you don't even want or need. That's not what we're doing here. Not even close. Because at this point in the book, your son has already:

- Been evaluated
- Found the right level
- Built a list of schools
- Sent personalized outreach
- Connected with coaches
- Delivered a great highlight video
- Followed up consistently
- Proven value on social media
- Been told by coaches that they're interested
- Been invited on a visit

This isn't a random pitch like everyone else. This is a relationship.

And when your son has done all of that, he's not even really "closing." He's simply nudging the coach to take the next step. To go from interested, to invested.

To go from considering, to committing. Just like they want your son to eventually do.

And that's where asking the right question becomes everything.

Not, "Can I have a scholarship?"

Not, "Will you offer me?"

But something more powerful.

Something that shows your son isn't begging. He's committed. And he's willing to earn it. That's what helped me earn my scholarship.

My mentor guided me through this process and helped me take the right steps at Ole Miss. Later, I looked back and reverse engineered what I did. I refined it.

I tested it with the athletes I've mentored from all over the country. And now it's a repeatable system that any athlete can use to confidently ask for the offer the right way.

That's how the ASK Playbook™ was created.

THE ASK PLAYBOOK™

Working toward an offer cannot be left up to chance. Your son needs to know what to say, when to say it, and how to say it, so that it leads to a real, committable offer.

The ASK Playbook™ comes into play after the visit, when interest is high, and it's time to move from conversation to commitment. Most athletes stall here. This is how your son keeps momentum and turns it into an offer.

THE ASK FRAMEWORK™

A – Assess the Relationship

Before asking anything, your son needs to know where things stand. Has the coach seen his film? Have they shown real interest? Has there been any communication beyond a camp invite or DM? Is your son on the coach's big board? And if so, where? Has he already been on a visit, or has he been invited to one?

If the answer is yes, he's in a position to move forward. If not, he needs to go back to building the relationship.

S – Show Up With Value

Your son should always come in with value first. This means keeping coaches updated on his progress, film, stats, and mindset.

He can't just ask for a scholarship. He needs to show he's improving, engaged, and serious. He needs to show the coach he understands their challenges and he has the ability to solve them. Tag coaches on social media. Send highlight updates. Stay top of mind. Don't disappear for weeks, then suddenly ask for an offer.

K – Know the Right Question

When the time comes, whether at the end of a phone call or campus visit, he needs to ask the right question:

"Coach, I'm really interested in your program. I'd love to be a part of it. What do I need to do to earn a scholarship?"

He's not asking for the outcome. He's asking for the process. This shows that you are willing to work for it, it shows confidence, and coachability. And it gives the coach permission to be honest about where he stands and what comes next.

You never want the runaround from coaches, and believe me, they'll give it to you. College coaches are the ultimate salespeople. If you let them smooth-talk you, you'll waste a ton of time chasing interest that was never going to turn into an offer.

Remember, college football today is a business. And if your son is the CEO of his own business, he has to ask the hard questions. That's how you avoid wasted time and get the result you want. Otherwise, you'll get pushed around.

Here's exactly how your son can implement this framework.

Step 1 - Know When to Ask

Don't lead with the ask. This should be the final question after a full conversation where your son has asked about:

- The program
- The position fit
- Where he stands on the board
- How the team recruits players at his position

All questions you learned in the last chapter. Only then, at the end of the conversation, should he ask:

"Coach, I really want to be a part of your program. What would I need to do to earn a scholarship?"

What if he is on a visit?

Then he should ask the question in person at the end of the visit. Not at the start of the conversation. Not in the middle. At the end.

What if he is on a phone call?

Same thing. Have your son ask after he's shown interest and asked the questions above. It should never feel like the only reason he called was to ask for an offer. It should always be the next logical question.

Step 2 - Don't Be Annoying, Be Persistent

If a coach says they'll follow up in a month, don't try to force it in a week. Instead:

- Keep tagging them in key updates on X (Twitter)
- Send updated film clips via DM, text, or email
- Stay visible, not clingy

Coaches will move on quickly if they feel like your son is too eager or trying to control the timeline.

Step 3 - Gauge Their Response

The way a coach responds to the "ask" will tell your son everything. There are now four types of responses:

A. The Offer

Coach says:

"We want to offer you a scholarship."

What it means: They're ready. The value has been proven. The relationship is strong.

What to do:

First, stay calm and thank the coach. Pretend like this happens all the time. Then ask the most important follow-up question:

"Is this a committable offer?"

Not all offers are created equal. Some are verbal, some are contingent, and some are "placeholder" offers. You need to know if your son could commit today if he wanted to.

If the offer is committable, congratulations! That's a huge win. But it's not time to stop yet, especially if this is your first offer. In fact, it's the starting point. Now it's time to build momentum.

Other great follow-up questions:

- *"What are the next steps if I want to commit?"*
- *"Is there a timeline you're working with for filling my position?"*

Then, no matter what, follow up in writing. A quick thank-you email or handwritten letter that confirms the conversation keeps everything professional and clear. Lastly, update your big board to move the school to the scholarship offer stage:

Interested Schools	Questionnaire Complete	Coaches Contacted	Coaches Responded	Area Coach ID	Calls Booked	Visit	Scholarship Offer
							Ole Miss

If the offer is not committable, then treat it as a Green Light and follow the process below.

B. The Green Light

Coach says:

"We're actually discussing it. Keep doing what you're doing."

What it means: Your son is on their board and in the conversation, but he's probably not in the top position on their board to get an offer yet.

What to do: Stay consistent. Keep performing and updating them weekly.

Follow-up questions to ask:

- *"What specifically can I work on and what do you need to see from me before you will be ready to offer?"*
- *"Should I plan a visit or keep sending updates for now?"*

These questions will let you know the validity of their statement and help move the coach from thinking about your son to acting on him.

C. The Yellow Light

Coach says:

"We like you, but we need to see ______ first."

What it means: Your son isn't ready, yet. But the door is open.

What to do: Write down exactly what they say. Then build a plan and follow through.

The most important thing your son can do at this moment is get a clear answer. Empty answers like "just keep grinding" or "we're watching" aren't helpful. If the coach doesn't give a specific next step, your son has to dig deeper and ask:

- *"What specifically can I work on and what do you need to see from me before you will be ready to offer?"*
- *"If I do that, would I be in the mix for an offer?"*
- *"What's the best way to send you an update when I've made progress?"*
- *"Would a visit help speed up that process?"*

This shows the coach your son is coachable, committed, and serious. Leaving the conversation without knowing exactly what to do next is the worst place to be. Your son needs clarity, and it's on him to respectfully ask for it. Remember, this is a business. Coaches will absolutely understand and respect your questions.

D. The Red Light

Coach says:

"We're full at your position right now."

What it means: They've filled their spots, or your son isn't a fit for what they need right now. The door is likely closed.

What to do: Stay respectful. Thank them for their time and honesty. Then mark them as lost or remove them from your Big Board and move on to the next school.

But don't just walk away empty-handed. This is still a chance to grow, gather information, and see if there may be an opening in the future. Have your son ask:

- *"Is there any specific reason I didn't fit what you were looking for?"*
- *"Can I stay in touch in case something changes?"*
- *"Do you know of any other schools still looking at my position?"*

Most athletes shut down after hearing a 'no.' But the best ones stay poised and professional. That keeps the door open, and makes coaches more likely to refer him to other programs. You'd be surprised, this happens all the time. Especially when a coach really likes your son. And if he follows this playbook to a T, they will.

The worst thing your son can do after a red light is go silent. The best thing he can do is stay classy, stay confident, and move forward. Because rejection isn't the end. For the right athlete, it's just the beginning.

FROM NOT YET TO A D1 OFFER

Keats Bohannon dealt with more rejection than most athletes ever will. Actually, I think he dealt with more than any other player I've mentored. Coach after coach told him no. Some said they were full. Others flat-out ignored him. And for most athletes, that's where it ends.

But Keats didn't fold. He used the ASK Playbook™. He tracked his outreach. Personalized every message. Followed up like clockwork. He moved quickly when coaches gave him a red light and leaned in when they showed interest.

And then, finally, he got a yellow light.

A Division 1 coach told him, "We like you, but we need to see more top-end speed." Most players would've said "Okay" and left it at that. Not Keats.

He asked the uncomfortable and tough follow-up questions that most players won't: "What 40 time do you need to see?" and "If I improve that and send updated film, would I be in the mix for an offer?"

And because he asked those questions, the coach gave him a target. Keats went to work. He trained harder. Got faster. And showed the coach his progress. Then because he received the coach's permission he followed up, relentlessly. And over time, the responses shifted.

The yellow turned to green. The green turned into an offer. Keats earned a Division 1 offer, not because of hype or connections, but because he followed the system, took action on the feedback, and refused to let a yellow light go dim. Your son can do the same.

KEY TAKEAWAYS

- Your son isn't begging when he asks. He's showing commitment, confidence, and a willingness to earn it.
- The ASK Playbook™ is how your son moves from "interest" to real, committable offers.
- The key question isn't "Will you offer me?" It's "What do I need to do to earn a scholarship?"
- Timing is everything. Don't lead with the ask. Ask at the end of a meaningful conversation or visit.
- There are four types of responses: Offer, Green Light, Yellow Light, and Red Light. Each one tells your son exactly what to do next.
- If a coach gives vague or non-specific feedback, your son must ask clarifying questions or he'll walk away without a clear path forward.
- Rejection isn't the end. It's the beginning for athletes who know how to respond and follow up.
- Great players earn scholarships by consistently proving value, and by knowing when and how to ask for what they've earned.

YOUR NEXT PLAY

1. Have your son role-play with his mentor or role-play with your son to prepare for the most important question he'll ask in the recruiting process using the ASK Playbook™. Practice how he'll ask the question during a visit or call.
2. Write down and have your son role-play the follow-up questions he can use in response to any answer—offer, green, yellow, or red.
3. If he gets an offer, confirm it's committable. Then follow up with gratitude.
4. If he gets a green light, continue to stay in communication. Ask for a visit and ask what you can do to put yourself over the top.
5. If he gets a yellow light, turn it into a checklist. Post it on the wall. Knock out every item and be sure to let the coach know as soon as you do.
6. If he gets a red light, move on with class, and send one final message that leaves the door open.
7. Then update his big board.

PLAY 12: NEGOTIATE THE OFFER

"The best outcome in negotiation is not I win, you lose. It's we both win."

CHRIS VOSS

It was a Saturday, the weekend before signing day and I was eating lunch when I heard a ding. I looked down at my phone. It was a text from Mrs. King, my client Cooper King's mom.

It said, "Richie…Cooper just got another offer. And this is the school we did an official visit to last weekend. We're super excited because it's the school he really wants to go to. But after they showed us the numbers, I don't think we'll be able to afford it."

My heart sank. Not because it wasn't a good offer. But because I've seen this exact moment take a dream away from too many families. They do everything right. They find the right school. The right fit. The right coaches. But then, even after a scholarship offer, the price tag hits, and it all falls apart.

I texted her right back. "Are you free for a quick call?" She replied immediately, "Absolutely." When I called, it wasn't just her. Her husband and Cooper were on the phone too. And you could hear it in their voices. They were excited and hopeful. This was the school Cooper had been dreaming about. It checked every box. They were all in.

But under the excitement, I could hear the hesitation. The school costs $30,000 per year. The athletic scholarship they offered was for $15,000. That meant Cooper's family would have to pay the remaining $15,000 each year, or $60,000 over four years. For some families, that just isn't realistic. And they don't want their sons to go into debt with student loans.

Mrs. King said softly, "We really want to make this work. But I just don't think we can swing it." I took a breath and said, "Don't worry. You don't have to walk away from this. This is exactly what I'm here for. There's a real chance we can get this closer to a full ride. But we have to move fast. And we have to do this the right way."

I asked her to walk me through the numbers. We talked through what was actually covered and what wasn't. We broke down the total cost. We looked at the offer from every angle and found out what was still on the table. And we started putting together a plan.

Then I helped them figure out just how serious this coach was about Cooper. Had the coach followed up after the visit? Was Cooper high on the school's big board? Had the coach given additional specific feedback, and checked in regularly? The answer to all of these questions was "yes". And that told me we had room to work.

So I shared with them exactly what they were going to say, line by line. I guided them through the exact words to use, what to say first, how to frame the ask, and how to close with confidence. Then we role-played it multiple times. I wanted them to sound confident, respectful, and clear. We practiced until it felt like a real conversation, not a pitch.

Then they picked up the phone and called the coach. 15 minutes later, they called me back. Mrs. King said, "He said the budget's already stretched. I don't think he can do anything." Her voice was flat. The energy was gone. You could feel it. Just 30 minutes earlier they were all lit up with hope, and now it felt like that dream was slipping away.

But I wasn't done. I'd been here many times before. When a coach comes back firm after the first ask, there's a process, a powerful second move. So I walked them through the Next Play. I showed them how to reframe the ask using Tactical Empathy. Then we role-played again.

Before they got on, I told them, "Text me while you're on the call. I'll be right here with you the whole time." And they did. While they were on the phone with the coach, they were also texting me in real time, every question and new response. I was coaching them through the negotiation live. That final call changed everything.

Just 30 minutes later, my phone buzzed again. I picked up and heard Mrs. King's voice break through the line. "Richie...he found $10,000 more per year." You could hear it, her voice was lit up. Shock. Joy. Relief…all at once. Then Mr. King jumped on. "He actually made it happen. We're at $25,000 now."

Cooper was right there too. He said, "Coach, thank you. I can't believe it." You could hear it in his voice. He wasn't just excited, he was proud. Because he knew he had earned this moment.

Cooper King's Family & Richie Contartesi

They were ecstatic. It was like the weight of the world had lifted off their shoulders. And then, on top of that, we uncovered another $3,000 in academic aid. That dropped their out-of-pocket cost to just $2,000 per year.

Let's break it down:

- Total cost: $30,000 per year
- Initial football scholarship: +$15,000 per year
- Additional aid after negotiation: +$10,000 per year
- Additional academic aid: +$3,000 per year
- Total aid package: $28,000 per year
- Remaining out-of-pocket: $2,000 per year

So instead of paying $60,000 over 4 years, they were only responsible for $8,000.

And that last $2,000 per year? Cooper could earn it back by retaking the SAT and raising his score just a few points. He started at a 50% offer and finished at 93%.

That wasn't luck. That wasn't some fancy trick. That was a family following a proven playbook, with a coach in their corner, that saved them $52,000 over four years. But of course, I didn't always know how to do this.

The first time I ever negotiated an offer, I was a senior in high school. JU, a small FCS program, had just offered me. I remember being so excited until I saw the numbers. It wasn't enough, not for what my family could afford.

I didn't want to lose the opportunity, but I had no idea what to say. That's when my mentor stepped in. He didn't tell me to beg, bluff, or push. He walked me through exactly what to say, how to say it, and why it mattered. We wrote it out, role-played it, and I made the call.

That one conversation increased the offer. Looking back, I'm grateful I had support and that I negotiated at all. Without that support, I would have owed even more. But I also know now that we left money on the table. I still had to take out a student loan. And that's exactly why I built the system I have today. So no athlete I mentor has to make the same mistakes I did or take on a large student loan.

Years later, after my football career was over and I'd started my own business, I studied *Never Split the Difference* by Chris Voss. I spoke with hundreds of college football coaches. And I built a system that combined everything I had learned, experienced, researched, and figured out during interviews with active coaches.

That's the same system Cooper's family used. And now, you'll learn it too.

Most families that reach out to me have no idea that getting the offer is just the beginning. Not because they did something wrong. But because no one ever told them. Cooper didn't just get lucky on signing day. He built leverage long before that, because he followed this entire playbook.

He targeted 60 schools. He reached out consistently. He stayed in touch with coaches. He built his brand on social media. He built real relationships. And because of that, he didn't just end up with one offer. He had several. And while you don't need other offers to negotiate successfully—which I will show you below—having them in your pocket makes the conversation a whole lot easier.

Think about your own career. If you've ever negotiated a salary for a new job, you know how powerful it is to have multiple offers on the table. It changes how you communicate. It changes how confident you feel. And it changes how the other side treats you.

This is no different. Recruiting is a business. And when you show up prepared, professional, and in demand, it puts you in control of the process, just like Cooper was.

Still, getting the offer is just the beginning. The real game starts when you understand how the money actually works, because not all offers are created equal.

Division I FBS offers are full rides because those programs have 85 scholarships. But some smaller FCS programs, and most D2 and NAIA schools, don't have that luxury. D2 programs only get 36 full scholarships to divide across the entire team. NAIA programs get just 24. So most offers at those levels are partial by design.

But what many families don't realize is that these offers are fully negotiable. And once you know how to stack the right kinds of scholarships, it gets easier and easier to close the gap and get closer to a full ride. Families often don't even know this is possible. Or they're afraid to ask. They think if they push too hard, the coach will pull the offer.

Coaches will never say it out loud, but negotiation is part of the recruiting process. Especially at the D2 and NAIA levels, where most scholarships are partial by design.

So what happens? They offer 25%. If you accept it right away, great. The coach couldn't be happier. But if you ask the right questions and follow the same system Cooper's family used, that 25% can turn into 50%, 90%, or even more.

This isn't about being pushy. It's not about being greedy. It's about understanding value. Your son has trained for this. He's earned the opportunity. And in many cases, the offer is flexible. But only if you know how to ask, when to ask, and what to say.

Because unlike football, where someone wins and someone loses, negotiation is not win-lose. It's win-win. Great negotiations help both sides get what they want.

Cooper's family didn't settle. They followed the process. They trusted the system. And they fought for the opportunity their son had earned. Today, Cooper is going to the school he loves and the football coach was able to get the player he wanted. Almost fully covered. Because his family was willing to do what most won't.

And if you don't negotiate? Someone else will. And that family will walk away with more scholarship money. We don't want that. Now it's your turn. Let me show you how to do the same thing.

THE NICE NEGOTIATION™ PLAYBOOK

The NICE Negotiation™ Playbook is how I help the players I mentor get the most out of every offer without ever being pushy. It's simple, clear, and it works.

N = Know the Offer

Before you can negotiate, you need to understand the full cost of attendance, exactly what's being offered, and what's not.

I = Interest Level

You only negotiate with coaches who are clearly invested. If the interest isn't there, you don't have leverage.

C = Communicate Value

This is where you show the coach why your son is worth more with updated film, leadership, offers, and progress.

E = Evaluate & Engage

Now you ask the right questions, handle the conversation like a pro, and make a confident decision based on all the data.

THE NICE FRAMEWORK™

N = KNOW THE OFFER

I = INTEREST LEVEL

C = COMMUNICATE VALUE

E = EVALUATE & ENGAGE

N = Know the Offer

Before you can negotiate, you need to know exactly what you're working with. Ask the coach these questions:

- *What is the total cost of attendance at your school?*
- *What percentage does the scholarship cover?*
- *Does it include tuition, fees, room, board, or books?*
- *Are there opportunities to increase the scholarship later?*
- *Can we stack academic, need-based, or external aid on top?*
- *How much time do we have to decide?*

This is your foundation. Write everything down. Make sure you understand what's covered now and what could be added later.

Now you need to determine your magic number. This is one of the most important numbers in the entire process. Your magic number is the amount your family can realistically afford to pay each year without going into debt, draining savings, or putting your future at risk.

For some families, that number might be $5,000 a year. For others, it might be $3,000 or less. Whatever it is, know it ahead of time. Why does this matter?

Because once you know your magic number, you'll know exactly how much more scholarship money you need to make the offer work for your family. That number becomes your target in the negotiation. And if a coach gets close to it, you'll have a powerful way to confidently close the deal—which you'll learn about soon.

One of the best ways to close that gap is through scholarship stacking. This is the concept of combining different types of aid on top of your football scholarship to reduce what you actually have to pay. This is exactly what Cooper's family did, and it changed everything.

Most D2 and NAIA programs use equivalency scholarships, which means they split their athletic money across multiple players. That's why stacking becomes such a powerful tool.

Here are the different types of scholarships to stack:

- Athletic aid – Based on performance and what was already offered to you
- Academic aid – Based on GPA or test scores
- Need-based aid – Based on your family's financial situation
- External scholarships – From local organizations or private sources
- Institutional aid – Extra money from the school itself

You will also ask the coach:

"Can we work with your financial aid office to explore academic or need-based stacking options?"

Scholarship Stacking Comparison Chart

Aspect	Division I (D1)	Division II & NAIA
Scholarship Types	Full (headcount sports) or partial	Mostly partial
Stacking Academic Aid	Allowed under strict NCAA rules	Freely allowed
Need-Based Aid	Can be added if total doesn't exceed COA (Cost of Attendance)	Can be stacked freely
Scholarship Limits	Strict limits for team scholarships	Greater flexibility in distributing aid
Recruitment Strategy	Attract top-tier athletes with full scholarships in headcount sports; stack aid for non-headcount sports	Combine athletic, academic, and need-based aid to build competitive packages

This is your foundation. Once you've gathered all the details and understand the full financial picture, you'll be ready to talk about interest. But before you do, never negotiate over text or DM. Always have the conversation in person. If that's not possible, pick up the phone.

This one move can completely change how seriously the coach takes your ask. It shows you're serious, and it gives you the space to actually talk through solutions. You can't do that in a text.

I = Interest Level

Now that you know where you stand, don't jump straight into money. First, you need to determine how serious the coach is about your son. Because if the coach isn't showing real, consistent interest, negotiating won't work. You'll either get ignored or shut down.

But if the coach is invested, if he sees your son as a true priority, then you have leverage. And in negotiating, leverage is everything.

So how do you figure that out? You'll start by asking the coach directly. If you're unsure how serious the coach is, don't guess, ask. These questions will give you clarity right away:

- "Where do I currently sit on your board for my position?"
- "Do you see me as a priority or a depth piece for this class?"
- "How many other players have committed at my position?"

When a coach gives you honest, specific answers, you'll know where you stand. If they stay vague or dodge the question, that's a sign they're not at 100%, and you shouldn't be negotiating yet. Next, measure their behavior, not just their words.

If a coach is truly invested, he won't just stay in touch, he'll go to bat for your son. That includes walking into the financial aid office himself, or even with you, to try and find more money. This happens all the time. In Cooper's case, once the coach saw how serious the family was about committing, he personally went and "found" the $10,000 more per year.

This kind of support only happens when the coach feels that your family is serious, professional, and prepared. It's the reward for asking the right questions, building real trust, and following this system.

Use the Coach Interest Score™ below to track what the coach is doing, not just what they say. This will help you decide whether to move forward with negotiating, or keep building the relationship first. Give the coach 1 point for each statement below that is true. Add up the total to calculate the Coach Interest Score.

Question	Yes = 1 Point
The coach has personally messaged or called your son multiple times	
The coach has watched your son's full highlight film	
The coach has asked for full game film	
Your son has been invited on an official or unofficial visit	
The coach has asked for transcripts or test scores	
The coach has introduced your son to coordinators or the head coach	
The coach has provided specific feedback (not just "looks good")	
The coach mentioned how your son fits into their system or scheme	
The coach has asked where else your son is getting interest or offers	
The coach has shared other offers and commitments at your son's position	

Score	Coach Interest Level	Negotiation Readiness
8–10	High	✅ Yes. You have leverage
4–7	Medium	⚠️ Maybe. Build more engagement first
0–3	Low	🚫 No. Focus on outreach and building trust

What to do based on your score:

- **8–10:** The coach is clearly interested. You've built enough trust and connection. You can move into the next phase of negotiation with confidence.
- **4–7:** You're getting close. Keep building the relationship. Share updated film. Stay consistent. Work to stack other offers for leverage.
- **0–3:** The coach isn't there yet. Focus your time on outreach and relationship-building. Don't try to negotiate. Just focus on moving up the board, and work to stack other offers for leverage.

If a coach hasn't shown strong, consistent interest, they're not ready to have a money conversation. You can't skip this step.

Build interest first. Then negotiate with power and leverage.

C = Communicate Value

This isn't about bragging. It's about making it clear why your son deserves more support. Whether your son has other offers or not, this step is critical. Coaches need to be reminded of his value, especially when you're entering a negotiation.

Here's how to do it:

- Send updated highlights or big plays
- Share leadership roles (captain, mentor, etc.)
- Show improved stats or grades
- Let the coach know other schools are offering
- Send testimonials or character references

Before you make the ask, use the first Chris Voss tactic, called Tactical Empathy, as the opening line. Acknowledge the coach's perspective first. This disarms tension and opens the door for a productive conversation. Say this first:

"Coach, I know scholarships aren't unlimited and you've got to balance a lot of players and needs. We really appreciate the opportunity."

If your son has other offers:

Let the coach know. It creates urgency and reinforces that your son is in demand. Say this:

"We really love what you're building here. We just wanted to be transparent that he's also received an offer from [School], and we're weighing all the options."

If he doesn't have other offers yet:

Focus on growth, momentum, and commitment. Say this:

"We're really excited about this opportunity. Since the season ended, he's made big strides, both academically and athletically. His [GPA or SAT/ACT score, etc.] has improved, and we just posted new highlights last week that show [what the coach is looking for]."

E = Engage with Confidence

Before you negotiate, double confirm what your magic number is and what you're willing to accept. What amount makes this doable for your family? What offer would make you say yes today? Get clear on that now, before you ever reach out. Because when you do ask, and the coach meets it, you need to be ready to commit.

Now you go right into the ask, but the right way. You'll ask:

"He's all in, but it is going to be tough financially. Would it be ridiculous to explore if there's any flexibility in the package?"

Then follow with:

Is there room to improve it a little?"

From there, based on how the coach responds, you can layer in these follow-up questions. Don't ask all at once, use what fits based on their response.

If you haven't already discussed scholarship stacking, ask:

"Would it be possible to explore academic or need-based stacking options with the school?"

Finally, use Loss Aversion to create respectful urgency. Loss Aversion is a cognitive bias in psychology and economics, where people perceive losses as having a greater psychological impact than similar gains.

In this case, you're working on a coach's psyche, by having him feel that the risk of losing out on the opportunity to offer your son is more emotionally painful than signing a similar player that he didn't "lose." Say:

"Coach, he really loves your program and this is his top choice. Another school did offer a higher package, so we're trying to see what's truly possible before making a final decision?"

Once you've made the ask, listen. Let the coach speak. Don't fill the silence. Just wait. Let them speak next.

When the coach feels your son is serious and your family is prepared, they may come back with a stronger offer, bring in financial aid support, or even find more money, just like Cooper's coach did.

Like mentioned earlier, knowing your magic number is critical. And if the coach hits your number? Be ready to say "yes". This is one of the most powerful moves you can make in a negotiation. It's called the Magic Number™ close:

"Coach, if we can get just $5,000 closer, we're ready to commit today."

That kind of clarity only comes when you've done the work. It shows the coach you're not shopping around. You're serious. And if he truly wants your son, he'll find a way to make it happen. You can close the deal right there. This is one of the most powerful ways to close a scholarship negotiation.

And if they don't, that's okay too. You'll walk away knowing you asked the right way and gave your son every opportunity he's earned. Stay respectful. Thank them and leave the door open:

"Coach, we really appreciate the offer and everything you've done. At this time, we're going to explore some other options. Thank you again for believing in him."

Being willing to walk away is powerful but absolutely keeps the door open. And remember, coaches talk. Stay professional. It matters. And in some cases the coach will realize you aren't bluffing and go "find" the money.

After all your negotiations, evaluate every offer side-by-side. To do that, you should create a simple spreadsheet that includes:

- Tuition covered
- Room and board
- Academic fit
- Playing time
- Distance from home
- Coaching staff and culture
- NFL pipeline or career support

Feel free to add any other variables that are important to you. This will help you make a clear, confident decision with your son and choose the right fit depending on your family's needs.

Cooper King's story isn't the exception. His family is just one I've helped negotiate scholarship offers. I've seen families reduce their cost from over $50,000 a year down to just a few thousand. I've seen late-round offers turn into full rides. And I've seen athletes just like your son go from overlooked to fully funded.

When you follow a proven playbook, and you're willing to ask the right way, you give your family a shot at the future you've worked so hard for.

KEY TAKEAWAYS

- A few smaller FCS programs, as well as most D2 and NAIA schools, offer partial scholarships by design. But that doesn't mean those offers are final.

- You must know the full cost of attendance and understand exactly what the offer covers.
- Your magic number is the amount your family can realistically afford per year. It's your guide in every negotiation.
- If a coach isn't truly invested in your son, you don't have leverage yet. Build the relationship and leverage first.
- When you're ready to negotiate, stack scholarship aid: athletic, academic, need-based, external scholarships, and institutional aid.
- The NICE Negotiation™ Playbook helps you stay confident, respectful, and get closer to what you deserve throughout the process.
- Coaches won't offer more unless you ask, and the best families ask the right way.
- Being ready to commit when your magic number is hit gives you a powerful close.
- If it doesn't work out, stay professional, stay respectful, and keep the door open, but be willing to walk away.

YOUR NEXT PLAY

- Calculate your family's magic number, the most you can afford to pay per year.
- Create a spreadsheet to compare all current and potential offers side by side.
- Use the Coach Interest Score™ to determine whether you're ready to negotiate.
- Follow the NICE Negotiation™ Playbook step by step with each coach.
- Role play and practice the ask out loud so you're confident when the moment comes.
- If the offer is close, use the Magic Number™ close: "Coach, if we can get just $___ closer, we're ready to commit today."
- If the coach can't meet your number, thank them and walk away with respect. Then move on to the next opportunity.

PLAY 13: TURN CAMPS INTO OFFERS

"Don't wait for an opportunity. Create it."

GEORGE BERNARD SHAW

I was sitting in the backseat of my mom's minivan as we pulled up to the camp. I looked out the window and saw hundreds of players all over the place. Some were stretching. Some already had their cleats on. Some looked like grown men.

My mom looked back at me with a smile and said, "Have a great time and kick butt." I looked at her nervously and said, "OK." Then I got out of the van.

She had worked all day and driven a few hours so I could chase a dream. But the truth is, we didn't even know if the coach had seen my film. We were spending time, money, and hope on a shot in the dark.

As I walked up to registration, there were so many players in line. When I got to the front, the staff barely looked at me. They scanned my name, handed me a shirt, and sent me through as fast as possible.

I found a spot on the grass and sat down. Coaches were standing around talking and laughing. A few players were walking up to them, shaking hands. But those guys looked like the big-time recruits. The ones who already had offers.

I didn't say anything. I just sat there, tied my cleats, and thought, "OK. I'll prove it on the field." The coaches called us into a circle and explained how the camp was going to work. Then we stretched, did warm-ups, and went through drill after drill. I was nervous, but I just focused on my next play. One play at a time.

During one-on-ones, I lined up against a big D1 cornerback. And I beat him. I thought for sure a coach would come talk to me after that. I kept looking around, waiting for someone to say something. But nothing happened.

Camp ended. Coaches were shaking hands and laughing with the "big-time" players. I just stood there, holding a T-shirt everyone was handed when leaving. No one talked to me. No one looked at me. Just a quiet "Thanks for coming."

I saw my mom's van pull up and I got in. She looked over and said, "How'd it go?" I said, "I think I did really good." She smiled and said, "That's awesome. We should be getting some calls now." But weeks went by and no calls came. No emails. No messages.

I went to more camps after that. Same story. I played hard. I competed. But every single time, I just went home with a T-shirt.

I thought I was making progress, but the truth is, I was falling behind. A camp without a coach who knows your name and has watched your film is just another paid workout. And unfortunately, this isn't just my story. It's the story I hear from almost every parent who reaches out to me today.

That's when I realized something was broken. Not just with recruiting camps, but with the whole approach. I believed that if I just kept going to camps, eventually it would work out. I thought if I just showed up and played well, the coaches would notice. I thought the invite meant something.

Most families think along the same lines. They show up and hope they get lucky, that the right coach will see them, just like I did. But like the theme of this book, hope is not a strategy. The truth is, camp invites don't mean anything unless the coach already knows who you are and has seen your game film.

Unfortunately, most camp invites are just marketing. They are not personal. They are not based on your film. They are just a way to fill up spots and collect registration fees. And the bottom line is, camps only matter after you've done everything else we've already talked about in this playbook:

- You've built your Big Board of your top 50 to 60 schools
- You've built your brand on social media
- You've done all the outreach
- And now you're getting interest and invites that actually matter

That's when a camp actually becomes an opportunity to secure an offer. It's really just another type of visit. And even if your son gets a random invite, he can still use the system I'm about to teach you to figure out if that camp is worth his time.

No more guessing or hoping. Every wrong camp you go to isn't just a waste of time. It's time you could have spent building a real relationship with the right coach. That's the real cost. Not the $100 camp fee, the hotel, or the travel. It's the $200,000 scholarship offer left on the table at the camp you should have been at.

FROMT-SHIRTS TO SCHOLARSHIP OFFERS

One of the first athletes I mentored was a wide receiver named Tyler. He had great hands, great effort, and zero offers. Just like me, he had gone to eight camps already and left with nothing but T-shirts.

When I looked at the schools he was targeting, I saw the real problem. He was aiming too high. Way too high. For example, if you are grading out as a Division II level player right now, but every camp you go to is a big-time Division I FBS school, you are going to walk away with a world of hurt. That is exactly what happened to me.

Your son is not invisible because he isn't talented. He's invisible because he's not on their board. And unless he's an absolute freak of nature, he's not going to end up there. That means running a 4.3 in the 40-yard dash, or being 6'5", 300 pounds, and throwing guys around like rag dolls.

I'm not saying your son can't work his way up once he's in college and transfer to a bigger program later. But when it comes to earning offers at camps, it doesn't work that way. You have to be on their board before you ever step on the field.

So this time, Tyler followed the process the right way. He executed what I teach in this playbook. We built his Big Board. We matched his level to the right schools. We did outreach the right way. And finally, the camp invites started rolling in. But this time, they came from programs that were actually a fit.

And instead of rushing to sign up like most families do, we followed a system. I used everything I had learned from my own recruiting mistakes. I combined it with what I later learned in business, from active college coaches, and what my mentor taught me.

I showed Tyler exactly how to respond to the coach's message. Not with blind excitement. But with confidence and a plan to make sure the invite could actually lead to an offer. And the next day, the coach replied and said, "We like your film. Let's hop on a call."

That one move changed everything. It proved the invite was real. It proved the coach knew who Tyler was. From there, Tyler got on a call with the coach and executed the entire pre-camp, camp, and post-camp playbook. The first camp didn't offer him on the spot. But the second one did. And so did the third.

Over that final summer before his senior year, Tyler earned three offers from six camps. That is a 50% conversion rate. That is when I knew the camp process works just like the recruiting process. It is just another step in the Offer Funnel™.

Some coaches will offer you based on your game film. Others will want to meet you in person to validate what they already believe. That was a massive mindset shift.

Recruiting camps are not something you go to in order to get exposure. They are just a tool. One tool in your tool belt to move coaches through the visit stage of the Offer Funnel™. Their main purpose is to validate a coach's belief about who you are so they can confidently offer you. That is the mindset shift.

Most families do not understand this. They go to camps thinking it will lead to exposure and a scholarship without coaches even knowing who their son is or having seen his film. But that is not how it works.

Unless your son is truly one of the top 2,000 players out of 1.1 million in the country, that approach will leave you empty handed. Yes, even if he beats out the so-called Division I prospects like I did.

You get exposure by doing outreach to the right schools in the right divisions.

You create interest by marketing yourself online and communicating confidently with those coaches.

You earn camp invites by targeting the right schools and sending your highlight video.

You validate those invites by speaking with coaches on the phone ahead of time to confirm they have actually watched your video and are actively recruiting you.

The only reason a coach invites you to a camp instead of offering you immediately is because they need to see it in person. Maybe it is a height check. Maybe it is speed. Maybe it is character or coachability. Whatever it is, they want to confirm what they already saw on film.

That is what camp is for. Not exposure. Confirmation and to earn the offer. That is the difference. That is why 50% of the camps Tyler went to resulted in scholarships.

Now, keep this in mind: You still have to perform well at these camps and prove what those coaches saw on film is real. But if you do exactly what I share in this chapter—before, during and after the camp—you can convert a high percentage of your camps into committable scholarship offers.

So while other parents waste time and money chasing exposure, I want you to shift your mindset. Think differently than every other parent. Start thinking of camp as a tool for confirmation. It is a validation step. And when you treat it that way, you give yourself the best chance to walk away with an offer.

Remember, there are a lot of different types of camps. I am not going to talk about skill camps in this chapter, because they have nothing to do with earning a scholarship. You can attend them, and in some cases you should, to improve your play on the field. But they are not recruiting camps, no matter how much they claim to be. As long as your expectations are clear that skill camps are purely for development, then whether your son attends them is up to you.

This chapter is about recruiting camps, specifically those held on college campuses where college coaches can legally attend, evaluate, and give offers.

Before we go deeper, let's simplify what you need to know. There are five main types of football recruiting camps. Here they are, ranked from worst to best when it comes to earning a football scholarship:

#5 — All-Star Games

These can be fun, and look great on social media. But no college coaches are allowed to attend, so there is no evaluation. That means no offers. Many of these games sound elite but are based more on revenue than recruiting. *(This does not include the Under Armour All-America Game or the Navy All-American Bowl.)*

#4 — Showcase Camps & Combines

These are great for getting testing numbers like your 40 time or vertical. Sometimes useful for 8th through 10th graders with no film. But no coaches can attend because they're not held on college campuses. Almost no one gets discovered at these unless they are already on recruiting boards.

#3 — 7-on-7 Tournaments

Fun for developing timing, routes, and confidence. But they are not real football. No linemen. No tackling. Coaches are usually not allowed to attend unless it's held on campus, which is rare. These events rarely lead to real recruiting outcomes, but can be great for skill development.

#2 — Mega Camps

Held on college campuses with coaches from many schools in attendance. These are better because coaches can legally evaluate and offer. But they are often overcrowded, and most coaches are only there to watch specific athletes who can't attend their school's individual college camp. These are suited for the top 2,000 players, and perhaps your son, if he is an absolute athletic freak of nature.

#1 — Individual College Camps

This is what this chapter is all about. These are camps hosted by one school and run by that school's coaching staff. When done correctly, this is the best chance to earn a real scholarship offer. But only if the coach already knows who your son is, has seen his film, and is bringing him in for validation.

The playbook I am about to share with you works for any of these camps, but the individual college camps are where you will earn the most offers. Now that you know what type of camp this chapter is focused on, let's walk through the exact steps to turn that camp into a committable offer.

It's called Camp Conversions™ and it is a seven-step playbook.

CAMP CONVERSIONS™

Each step matters. Each one builds on the last. And if you skip any of them, you risk leaving the camp empty handed.

Step 1: Respond to the Coach

You get camp invites by doing outreach to schools that fit your level of play. That's why knowing the right divisions to target is critical.

When those invites from the right schools start coming in, the first step is all about validating whether the invite your son received is real. I cannot stress this enough. Just because a coach sends a camp invitation does not mean they are actively recruiting your son. Camp invites are often mass-mailed to thousands of players, especially if you filled out a questionnaire or sent your film without a clear relationship in place.

With that said, it is a great way to start a conversation and relationship. Before you spend a dollar or book any travel, you must confirm interest. Here is how we do that.

Use this exact message before registering or making travel plans:

Coach (LAST NAME), Thank you so much for inviting me to the camp at (SCHOOL). I am really interested in the program and I definitely want to attend the camp, but I have a few questions before making the (___-HOUR) trip. Do you have a minute for a quick call? My number is (XXX) XXX-XXXX. You can quick call me or let me know when you're free. I'm excited about the opportunity.

If you don't hear back within a week, it could be an indicator that the coach isn't interested. But in most cases, the coach is just busy. Just like I shared with you in earlier chapters, the money is in the follow-up. That still holds true here. Most players never follow up, and that is one of the biggest mistakes you can make.

With that said, if no coaches are responding to your original response or follow-up, then you are probably targeting the wrong divisions and schools altogether. That is a sign you need to re-evaluate your Big Board and make sure your son is aligning with the schools that match his level and film.

Here's the follow-up message to send, if you don't get a reply, one week later:

Coach (Last Name), Thank you again for the camp invite. Definitely excited about it. Of course, as I'm sure you can understand, I'm trying to make smart decisions about which camps to attend for travel purposes. Are you available for a quick call to discuss your camp and the opportunity? My number is (XXX) XXX-XXXX.

Make sure to follow-up at least three times before moving on from the camp opportunity. What happens next will tell you everything. Here are three common coach responses and what each one really means:

Example 1:

"Hey JOHNNY, great to hear from you. Yes, we've seen your film and like what you bring to the table. You're someone we're tracking for the 2026 class. Let's hop on a call, I'm free after practice tomorrow around 6:30 PM. Sound good?"

What it means: This is real interest. They know who your son is. The coach has watched his film and is actively recruiting him. This is a green light to continue.

Example 2:

"Appreciate you reaching out. The best way to get evaluated is to come compete at camp. We'll be looking at all the guys who show up."

What it means: This is a generic response. No relationship has been built. If your son goes, he'll just be a number. This is not worth the time. Your time is much better served continuing to do outreach and find coaches who want you.

Example 3:

"Thanks for the message and interest, JOHNNY. Right now we're focused on finishing up our 2026 class, so we're not evaluating 2027s yet. Might be a better fit for next summer."

What it means: The coach is being honest and respectful. They are not recruiting your son right now. That may change later, and your son saved a trip by asking up front. But now your son can respond to the coach and ask if it's okay to share his game film and progress for consideration next year. Never leave a coach's message unanswered.

This one step can save your family thousands of dollars and months of wasted effort. It also helps your son show maturity and professionalism, traits coaches value highly. And best of all, if the coach is genuinely interested, this message starts the relationship off on the right foot.

Step 2: The Phone Call Script

When a coach agrees to hop on a call, that is a big win. But what you say on that call matters just as much. This is not a time for your son to pitch himself. It is a time to truly validate the camp invite, ensure they have watched his game film, start building the relationship, and see if an offer is a real possibility by asking the right questions. And the coach actually getting on the phone tells you a lot.

Make sure to have your son role-play this with you or his mentor 15-20 times before just jumping on a call with a coach. You would never run out on game day without preparing. Treat this the same way.

Here is the script to follow:

Coach (Last Name), thanks again for jumping on the phone. I really appreciate the invite to your camp and your time today. It means a lot.

I've been learning more about (School Name) and your program. I really like the way you guys play and how you develop players.

Then ask these three questions in this order:

1. *What's something you guys are really looking for in a player at my position?*
2. *What's one thing I should focus on this offseason to improve as a player?*
3. *As for your program, am I currently being evaluated or am I currently on your board? Where do I stand at this point?*

These questions do a few important things. First, they show you are serious about your development and that you really want to know what they are looking for to see if you are a good fit.

Second, they allow the coach to give specific feedback on your game film so you can confirm they watched it and they like it.

And third, they provide information you need to know, like whether they are actually recruiting you, and whether this camp is worth your time.

Most importantly, these questions help you shift from being just a name on a list to a real person the coach remembers and is evaluating.

Step 3: Set the Post-Camp Meeting

Now here is the secret. Before you end the call, it is important to schedule a time with the coach for after the camp to get feedback. This one step is critical to setting yourself up to ask for the offer and it shows confidence as well as a desire to improve. It also gives your son permission to speak with the coach after the camp without feeling forced.

Here is exactly what to say at the end of the call:

"Coach, real quick, at the end of the camp, would it be okay if I spent just one to two minutes with you to get your feedback on how I did?"

It is really important you ask this specific question. You are not asking for a meeting or for 30 minutes of their time. You are just asking for feedback. Coaches always say yes to this question, and getting permission to meet is one of the biggest advantages you can create for yourself.

Most athletes leave the camp and just walk to their cars holding a T-shirt, wondering what to do next. Your son will leave with the next steps. That "yes" from the coach sets the stage for everything that happens next.

At most camps, only a handful of players actually introduce themselves to begin with. Even fewer follow up afterwards. By setting this quick meeting ahead of time, coaches know who your son is beforehand and they'll be expecting to talk again when the camp ends.

This is how great relationships with coaches begin. Not by showing up and hoping to be noticed like everyone else. But by confidently communicating, leading the conversation, and asking smart questions at the right time.

Step 4: Introduce Yourself to All Coaches

The moment your son arrives at camp, his focus should be simple, go introduce yourself to the coaches. Don't wait for the perfect time. Don't look around for someone to go with. Don't hesitate.

One way I explain it to the athletes I mentor is by comparing it to walking up to a girl at a party. You can sit around all night, trying to time it perfectly, waiting for the crowd to clear or the music to change. But by the time you work up the courage, someone else already did it. And now you are stuck watching from the sideline, wondering what could have happened.

Plus, you get the hard part out of the way right from the start. You don't have to think about it all camp, and you don't give yourself time to overthink or talk yourself out of it.

Again, you want to execute Steps 1 through 3 before the camp. But if you weren't able to, you can absolutely still start the process here at Step 4.

If you already spoke with the coach on the phone, you definitely want to go straight to them and introduce yourself in person using the script below. But instead of asking the questions, bring up something specific from your phone conversation.

If you didn't speak with them beforehand, walk straight up to the first coach you see, shake his hand firmly, and say:

"Coach [Last Name], my name is [Your Name]. It's great to meet you! I'm really excited to be here at [Camp Name]. What position do you coach at [School]?"

Then follow up with these simple questions, in order:

1. *"How long have you been at [School Name]?"*
2. *"What are you looking for in players at my position at this camp?"*

If you already booked the post-camp meeting during your call with the coach, this is the time to simply remind them. You don't need to ask again. Just say:

"Coach, I'm fired up to show you what I can do today. I look forward to connecting after camp for one to two minutes to get your feedback."

If you didn't set the meeting beforehand, this is your chance to ask. Just say:

"I'm fired up to show you what I can do today. Would it be okay to connect for one to two minutes after the camp to get your feedback?"

These questions do a few powerful things. First, they help your son relax because these are simple questions that he can ask, and they are easy to answer for the coach. Once he's introduced himself to one coach, he'll have the confidence to talk to others.

Second, it shows the coaches that your son is mature and really wants it. Out of hundreds of players at most camps, only 10% or so introduce themselves to coaches. That's what makes it such an advantage.

Most athletes stay in their comfort zone. They sit, wait, stretch, and hope to get noticed. But your son is going to take control. By confidently walking up, shaking a coach's hand, and starting a conversation, he's already standing out before the first whistle blows.

Before you go to camp, make sure your son practices this exact conversation with you or his mentor 15-20 times. Practice the conversation as well as the handshake. A confident, firm handshake is an excellent way to set the tone.

It is also important that your son is prepared to answer questions. Make sure he reviews the commonly-asked questions and his answers from the Visits chapter, and role-plays those answers ahead of time. Practice just like he would before a game. Because when he gets it right, it removes all the pressure and sets the tone for the rest of the camp.

Step 5: Stand Out During Camp

Now that the introductions are out of the way, it is time for your son to perform. This is where most players try to "flip the switch." But standing out at camp is not just about making a few great plays. It is about showing consistency, effort, focus, and coachability from start to finish, as well as validating what the coach needs to see to offer your son. I am not going to go into too much detail here because this book is specifically about earning a scholarship, but here are a few things the athletes I mentor use to dominate at camps.

College coaches are watching more than just how fast your son runs or how high he jumps. They are watching how he warms up. How he listens. How he responds to coaching. And how he treats other players.

The first thing your son should do is get to the front of the line during every warm-up and drill. This shows leadership and confidence. He does not have to be loud or flashy. Just show up ready to work and lead by example.

Second, help him focus on just one play at a time. One drill at a time. He should not worry about what is coming next or get distracted by other players or who is watching. His mindset should be, "All I have to do right now is dominate this one rep, then the next, and then the next."

For example, he should not worry about one-on-ones when he is in individual drills. Just execute the next play in front of him to the best of his ability. When he does that, great results will follow.

Third, make sure he keeps his energy high and his attitude positive. Coaches are drawn to players who bring great energy. If he messes up, he should own it and move on to the next play. If another player makes a big play, he should encourage them. This shows maturity and team-first character.

Do not let him sit back. He should get as many reps as possible. One of the players I mentored followed steps 1 through 4 and performed well at camp. And the final reason the coach pulled the trigger and offered him was because they had a coach counting reps.

They were watching to see which players stayed in the back and which ones went all in. He had the most reps out of everyone and that rep count is what pushed the coach over the edge to offer him.

College coaches call this "the juice." It is so important that your son shows them he has the juice.

Fourth, make sure your son shows coachability. When a coach gives feedback, he should respond with eye contact and say, "Yes, Coach." Then apply the correction on the next rep and then follow up with the coach so he knows he corrected it. Coaches want players who can take direction and improve quickly.

Finally, remind your son that camp is not the time to try and be someone he is not. He does not need to wear neon cleats or be loud if that's not who he is. Your son already started standing out the second he responded to the invite and introduced himself to a coach. And if he followed steps 1 through 4, the coaches are already watching him.

Step 5 is where he proves that everything they saw on film is real. And when he does that, he sets himself up to ask the most important question.

Step 6: Ask For The Offer

This is it. Now is the time to cash in. Your son has a built-in reason to go talk with the coach again. Your son will leave with real feedback and possibly a path to an offer.

Right after the camp is over, your son should walk straight up to the coach, give a firm handshake, look him in the eye, and say:

"Hey Coach (Last Name), remember when we spoke earlier and I asked if I could get your feedback after the camp? I really enjoyed being here and want to find ways to keep getting better. What were your thoughts on the camp and how I performed today?"

If he didn't get a chance to book that meeting earlier, that's okay too. He should still walk up to the coach confidently and say:

"Coach [Last Name], thanks again for taking the time to speak with me at [Camp Name]. I really enjoyed being here. What were your thoughts on the camp and how I performed today?"

Then your son should ask the following questions in order. These are designed to give clarity, build the relationship, and open the door to an offer:

1. *"What's one thing I should focus on this offseason to improve as a player?"*
2. *"Based on what you saw today, where am I on your board?"*

If the coach gives great feedback and it sounds like your son is high on the list, now is the time to ask:

"Coach (Last Name), I really enjoyed being here and I love your program. What do I need to do to earn an offer?"

If the coach does offer your son, follow the post-offer process from the "Ask for the Offer" chapter.

If the coach doesn't offer on the spot, your son should immediately follow up with this:

"What specific things can I work on to earn (an offer or a spot on your board)?"

It is important that the coach's answer is specific. If the feedback is vague, your son should respectfully ask for clarity so he can take action and follow up later.

Lastly, make sure your son gets direct contact info if he doesn't already have it. He can say:

"What's your cell phone number so I can send you my film today?"

Confidence is key here. If your son wants the coach's number, he needs to ask for it directly. That one simple question can be the start of a long-term recruiting relationship. Don't ask for an

X handle either. And if that's all the coach gives, it tells you how serious they are about recruiting your son at this time.

Practice this conversation just like any game-day scenario. Have your son role-play each question and answer with his mentor or with you 15-20 times. The more he practices, the more confident and natural it will feel. And when done well, this step can turn a camp into a committable offer or concrete next step toward earning an offer.

Step 7: Post-Camp Follow-Up

No matter how well your son plays or how well he follows the system, not every camp will end with an offer. Some coaches just are not ready to pull the trigger for any number of reasons.

In the last step, your son did a good job of finding out what that reason might be. But without the follow-up, all of it becomes a giant waste. This is your son's chance to show the coach how badly he wants it by taking action and improving on whatever the coach told him.

So as the theme continues throughout this playbook, the money is in the follow-up. What your son does after camp is just as important as what he did during the camp. This is how he keeps the momentum going and stays top of mind with coaches who are evaluating hundreds, if not thousands, of athletes every single week.

He should follow up with the coach at least 3-5 times over the next 3-5 weeks. This keeps your son top of mind without being pushy and shows coaches he is serious, consistent, and coachable.

If your son just leaves camp and waits, he'll quickly be forgotten. But if he follows up the right way, he can stand out as someone who belongs at the next level.

Your son should send a short, professional DM, text, and email within 24 hours of the camp. That means sending the same message as an email, DM, and text. If he had a post-camp meeting with the coach, this message should reference that conversation. If not, it should highlight his excitement and show his willingness to improve.

Template:

Subject: *(Camp Name)*

Coach (Last Name),

Thank you for taking the time to speak with me at (Camp Name).

I learned a lot from the experience and am even more excited about the possibility of [potentially being a part of your program/visiting your school/meeting the team] because [Insert something specific about the offense, defense, or culture].

I look forward to (Next Step You Discussed At Camp).

(End with a question about setting up a visit, next steps, or discussing the opportunity.)

Example questions:

- *What are the dates available for a visit?*
- *When is a good time to discuss the next steps in the recruiting process?*
- *How did your conversation go with the head coach?*

This message does a few critical things:

It reminds the coach who your son is. It shows gratitude and professionalism. It references specific details about the program, and it proposes a clear next step to keep the relationship alive.

Most players never do this. And those who do often just send a generic "Thanks, Coach" message with no direction.

Your son is different. He is playing the long game. And this message keeps him in the conversation while others fade away.

If the coach gave feedback at the camp, your son should also reference that feedback in another follow-up message 2-3 weeks later, after he's worked on it. Here is an example:

"Coach, I appreciated the advice about improving my lateral speed. I've been working on it with my trainer and would love to show you my updated film when it's ready. Thanks again for your guidance."

That kind of follow-up stands out in a big way. Coaches remember that. And coaches can only offer players they know and remember.

FROM CHINA TO A D1 OFFER

One player I will never forget is CJ Cheng. He was not your typical recruit. He lived in China and had never played football in the United States. He didn't even have game film from an American high school. All he had was a dream, some Chinese game film, and an Instagram account.

When CJ first messaged me, I thought it was a scam. He sent me DMs on Instagram again and again. I didn't reply at first. But he kept showing up. Finally, I answered and took a leap of faith by jumping on a Google Meet with him. After a few conversations, I realized this kid was for real, and serious.

His dream was to play college football in the United States. He had no connections. No exposure. Nothing but game film from his high school in China and a hunger to do whatever it takes. So I decided to take the risk and bring him on as a client. We got right to work.

We mapped out the right schools based on his level of play. We created a camp schedule, and then he followed the Camp Conversions™ playbook step by step. Every step I shared with you in this chapter is the exact system CJ followed.

And guess what? CJ earned a Division I offer. He came all the way from China. He had no U.S. game film. He had never played a down of American football. But by following this playbook, he built real relationships and put himself in position to get a D1 offer.

If CJ can do it with a heavy Chinese accent, your son can too. That's the power of executing this system. That's the power of doing the work. That's the power of follow-up.

KEY TAKEAWAYS

- A camp is not only where your son gets discovered. It's where he gets validated.
- The only reason a coach invites your son to camp instead of offering right away is because they need to validate something in person.
- Most camp invites are just mass marketing. If the coach doesn't know your son by name or hasn't watched his game film beforehand, it isn't real interest yet.
- The Camp Conversions™ system gives your son a step-by-step plan to turn camp invites into committable offers.
- Executing each step before, during, and after the camp is how your son stands out and moves up the board.
- Your son should never register for a recruiting camp until he confirms that the coach has seen his film and is actively recruiting his position.
- The follow-up is just as important as the camp itself. Most players skip this. Your son won't.
- Your son will now leave the camp with either a scholarship offer or exactly what he needs to do to earn one.

YOUR NEXT PLAY

- Review the Camp Conversions™ system with your son. Go through the seven steps together.
- Role-play the phone script.
- Role-play the camp scripts.
- Review the camp invites he's received and use Step 1 to validate them.
- Use this system to create his camp schedules moving forward.

PLAY 14: THE SECRET PLAY

"You miss 100% of the shots you don't take."

WAYNE GRETZKY

It was a hot September afternoon in Texas. The sun was beating down, and the heat seemed to rise off the pavement in waves. That late-summer kind of heat, the kind that makes the air feel heavy, like time is running out.

My phone rang and it was Narci's mom.

She sounded tired, frustrated, and worn thin. And you could hear it in her voice, she was trying to hold it together. "Richie," she said, "he's done everything on the field. He's been working his tail off for years. I thought coaches would be reaching out by now. What are we missing?"

As you already know at this point, I hear this every day. A good kid. With great parents. But no traction. No offers.

Narci Wickley was a hard-hitting defensive player. He had heart, toughness, and game film to back it up. He wasn't flashy. He wasn't loud. But he was a dog. The kind of kid who doesn't just play the game, he lives for it.

Unfortunately, Tarleton State wasn't calling. And that was his dream school. It had everything. Right athletic level. Right location. Right system. Narci wasn't just interested, he was all in. But no matter what he did, the coaches at the school weren't responding.

When I first spoke to Narci, I could hear it in his voice. He wanted this badly. But he'd made the decision to go all in on college football late, and that meant he was starting from behind.

So I told him the truth. "You're behind. But you're not done. If you follow this playbook and you don't skip any steps, we can still make this happen."

And that's exactly what he did. We got to work. My team did a professional evaluation of his game film and re-ordered his highlight video. Narci graded as an FCS-level player. But it was already his senior year. And in recruiting, senior year means time is running out.

Still, we didn't waste a second. Narci followed the playbook to the letter. He sent emails. Made calls. Posted content. Did outreach. He followed up. He built his Big Board. He executed without excuses and offers started coming in.

A few NAIA. A couple from solid D2 schools and one from Lamar, a D1 FCS program. But Tarleton? Nothing. Not even a "no."

And in some ways, that's worse. Because at least when you get a no, you can mark the school as lost on your big board and move on. With no responses, you don't know what to think. You just have to keep trying.

That's when I sat down with Narci and told him straight up, "This is why we target 50 to 60 schools. Because even when you're a perfect fit, some coaches just aren't ever going to respond. You slip through the cracks."

He looked at me and said, "Coach Richie, I am thankful for the other schools, but this is the one I want."

And I believed him. So I said, "Then it's time."

He said, "Time for what?" I smiled. I said, "Time to walk in the front door."

He blinked, unsure. "You mean…drive there? In person?"

"Yes," I said. "When all else fails, this is the "secret" play. Not to beg. Not to ask for the offer. But to walk in with confidence and ask for just two minutes.

I walked him through the entire playbook in this chapter. Every step. No guesswork. Just execution. He looked at me, nodded, and said, "Let's do it."

That next morning, Narci and his mom got in the car. He packed his iPad with his highlight video cued up and ready to go. We printed his transcripts, letters of recommendation, everything. Five hours on the road. No guarantee. No invitation. Just preparation, heart, and belief.

Before they arrived, he followed my instructions. "When you get close," I said, "stop at the nearest donut shop. Grab a big box and bring them with you. Trust me, the law of reciprocation works. Especially when you're walking in cold and nobody knows who you are."

It's like what my daughter Carmella does to me all the time. She'll draw me a picture or bring me something I like, look up at me with those big eyes, and say, "Here Daddy, I got this for you." And five seconds later, "Can we get ice cream?" And yup, she gets me. Every. Single. Time.

That's how the law of reciprocation works. Give first. Then ask.

We role-played what he was going to say 15 times. The intro, the pitch, his tone, and the confidence. Until it was locked in. He walked through the doors, box of donuts in hand, and approached the front desk.

The woman behind the desk looked up and smiled. "Are these for us?" He grinned. "Absolutely."

She laughed. "Thank you! But, who are you?" Narci looked her in the eye and said, "I'm glad you asked. My name is Narci Wickley. And I'm your new edge rusher."

Then he asked to speak with the Director of Player Personnel. When the coach came out, Narci was ready. iPad in hand, highlight video queued up, nerves steady.

He stood tall, looked the coach in the eye, shook his hand and said, "Coach [Last Name], thank you for taking a few minutes. I just drove five hours to be here. I'm not asking for a scholarship. I'm not even asking for a spot. All I'm asking for is two minutes to watch my highlight video and let me know if there's any potential interest for the future?"

The coach nodded, donut in hand. Narci tapped play. 90 seconds in, the coach leaned forward and said, "Come with me. Let me grab the D-Line coach."

He led Narci down the hall into the defensive line meeting room. The lights were low. The D-Line coach was already there, sitting in the dark, watching film.

The D-line coach looked up and said, "What's up?" The recruiting coordinator said, "I just saw this player's video, and I think you need to see it. ASAP." "Alright," the D-Line coach said. "Throw it on."

Narci pressed play again. About ninety seconds in, the D-Line coach leaned back and said, "Let me get the Defensive Coordinator."

A few minutes later, the Defensive Coordinator walked in. Both coaches looked at him and said, "Watch this." Narci hit play one more time.

Now he was sitting in front of three coaches, all watching his film, one after another. Just like I explained earlier in this book, this is how the recruiting ladder works. The area coach watches first. If he gives the green light, the film goes to the position coach. Then to the coordinator. And finally, the coordinator or head coach signs off.

But when you're running the secret play, it happens fast. I mean much faster. Live and in real time. Narci stayed calm, even though the excitement in the room was building. His heart was racing, but on the outside, he stayed cool, confident, and collected.

He knew this was the moment. We had walked through this exact scenario together multiple times. Then the Defensive Coordinator looked over and said, "Tell me, Narci…who are you?" That was his cue.

He stood tall and delivered his pitch. The one we had practiced what felt like a million times. Word for word. Eye contact. Controlled tone. No rambling. No nerves. Just confidence.

He told them exactly how he fit their defense. How he could solve a real problem for them on the field. And then he made it personal. He shared why he wanted to be at that school, not just for football, but for his future. And that's what really got their attention.

But then the room got quiet. The Defensive Coordinator sat in silence, just staring at Narci and his mom. Seconds felt like minutes. Finally, the defensive coordinator leaned forward and said something Narci told me he will never forget.

"I wish more players at this level had the guts to do what you just did. I have a lot of respect for you, Narci. Your film is exactly what we're looking for. And the guts it took to show up like this, that's the type of character and player we want in our program."

He then asked, "Are you planning on transferring or being here all four years?" Narci replied, "No, Coach. This is where I want to be."

Before he said anything else, the coach looked at Narci and asked, "Do you have your transcript with you?"

Narci nodded yes because he was prepared. He reached into his folder and handed it over without missing a beat. The coach read through it for what felt like an hour.

The Defensive Coordinator paused. "We want to offer you. And if you come in and do what I think you can do, you're going to have a great career here."

Without missing a beat, Narci looked him in the eye and said, "Coach, I will not let you down. You just made one of the best decisions of your coaching career."

The coach smiled, then laughed. "Alright then. Prove it."

Think about that. This was a school that hadn't responded to a single email, message, or phone call. Narci had reached out again and again. Nothing.

But that day, because of what he did and how he did it, he walked away with a Division 1 offer at his dream school. It didn't happen by luck. It happened because he put in the work ahead of time.

He got professionally evaluated to make sure he went to a school at the right level. He built a highlight video that grabbed attention in the first 30 seconds.

He spent months practicing his pitch, crafting it, refining it, role-playing it until it rolled off his tongue with confidence. He developed the habits, the mindset, and the courage to walk into that building ready to compete.

And in the end, it all paid off. Narci sat in that meeting room with three high-level coaches and backed up his highlight tape with unwavering confidence. The coaches saw it. They felt it. They couldn't let him walk out of that building and end up at another program.

If Narci had skipped one step, if he hadn't done the prep work, the research, the reps, he probably would've walked out with nothing. But instead, he walked out with an offer.

He didn't wait for someone to save him. He didn't sit around hoping to be seen. He showed up with a plan. And when every door shut, he walked in the front one.

And that's why this chapter exists. What Narci did wasn't luck or magic. It was a process. A step-by-step play that many athletes I've mentored have used to create the same or similar results.

THE FACE PLAY™

I call it the FACE Play™. And when all else fails, you can always show up in person. Here's how it works:

F = Find the Right Fit

Target a school where your film matches the level and the need. Know the coaches. Know the scheme. Know where you fit both on and off the field.

A = Arrive Prepared

Bring your highlight video on a device ready to play, your transcripts, and letters of recommendation. Dress sharp. Be early. Practice your pitch. And yes, bring donuts.

C = Connect with Confidence

Ask to speak with the Director of Player Personnel. When they say yes, press play. Show them your film. Then deliver your pitch, explain how you fit their system, and tell them why you want to be at their school.

E = Elevate the Moment

If they respond well, ask clear follow-up questions, get their cell phone number, and confirm the next step. Then send a handwritten thank-you note to leave a lasting impression.

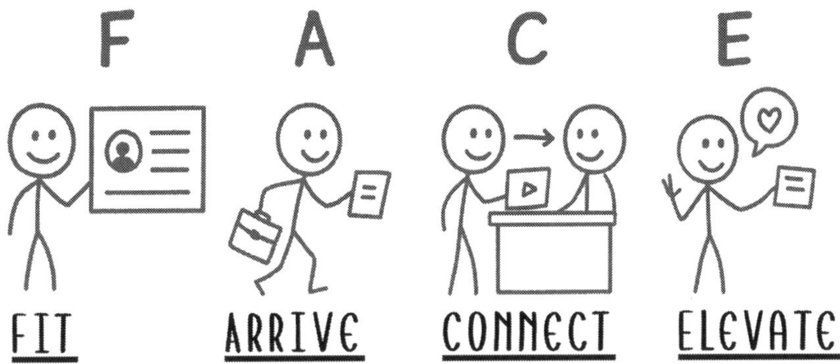

Now, here's exactly how to run the play and walk in the front door the right way:

F = Find the Right Fit

This step is non-negotiable. Walk in unprepared, and you walk out empty-handed.

Target Schools: Get a professional evaluation and target a school where your film matches the level and the need. Know the coaches. Know the scheme. Know where you fit.

Highlight video: Downloaded on your tablet or laptop, or saved in the photos section and ready to play with one tap. No loading. No buffering. The first 30 seconds must be strong enough to hook a coach immediately. You don't get unlimited time.

Most coaches will give you two minutes, max. If you're fumbling with the Wi-Fi or trying to pull it up on your phone, they'll say something like, "Just email it to me and I'll watch it later." You've lost the moment. Be ready on the spot.

Transcripts: Printed and ready to hand over any time.

Letters of recommendation: From coaches who can speak to your character, performance, and work ethic.

Appearance: Dress clean. Look confident. No sandals or wrinkled T-shirts. Dress to impress.

Research: Before you go, study the team. Try to watch recent games on YouTube or online. If film isn't available, read coach interviews, team previews, read coach's bios or social media to learn how they describe their offensive or defensive scheme. The goal is to understand how you fit before you even walk in the door.

Donuts: Yes, bring donuts. It breaks the ice, makes the front office smile, and shifts the energy before you even say a word.

Timing: Do not go during the NCAA dead period. You can visit during quiet, contact, or evaluation periods, but dead periods mean no in-person contact is allowed. The best time to go is early morning, around 8 AM to 9 AM, when coaches are fresh and still in the building.

I don't make a big deal of these periods throughout the book because everything else we do with outreach, social media, and follow-ups can be done anytime. When it comes to visits, coaches will give you the dates. But for this strategy, if you show up during a dead period, you'll be completely shut down. Nobody will meet with you. No film will be watched. You'll waste the trip. Here's what those periods mean for full context:

- Dead Period: No in-person contact with coaches at all, not on or off campus.
- Quiet Period: You can visit the school and talk to coaches, but they can't come see you play.
- Contact Period: Coaches can meet with you in person, visit your home, or come to your games.
- Evaluation Period: Coaches can watch you play and visit your school, but can't talk to you in person off-campus.

Before your son leaves home, just like always, make sure to role-play his entire pitch with his mentor or you 15-20 times. Practice your tone. Rehearse your handshake. The goal is to walk in looking like a future leader, not a lost recruit.

A = Arrive Prepared

When you arrive, your body language is critical. Walk in with your chest up, shoulders back, and a smile. Move with intention. Do not walk in slowly or look unsure. And whatever you do, do not ask for the head coach, a coordinator, or even your position coach.

Walk up to the front desk and say:

"Hi, My name is (Your Name) and I'm your new (your position). Could I please speak with the Director of Player Personnel (or Director of Recruiting?)"

These are the people who can evaluate film first, besides the area coach, and are usually in the building. They're the gateway. They're also the most likely to be available, especially when position coaches or coordinators are traveling or out on the road recruiting.

When they come out, don't pitch right away. Have your ipad or laptop ready. Smile, shake their hand firmly, and say:

"Coach [Last Name], thank you for taking a few minutes. I just drove/flew [X] hours to be here. I'm not asking for a scholarship or a roster spot. I'm just asking for two minutes of your time to watch my highlight video and let me know if there's any potential interest for the future?"

Make sure to elevate your tone at the end so they know it is a question.

C = Connect with Confidence

Once they agree, and they will if you follow that script word for word, press play.

While the video plays, stay quiet. Don't narrate. Let the film speak. Wait for them to talk first. If they have any interest, they'll lead you to the next step in their recruiting process or start asking more about you. That's your cue. Now it's time to begin your pitch.

Template:

"Coach, I've done my homework on your program and your system. I know you run a [defensive or offensive scheme], and I play [position]. Based on what I've studied, I believe I can help your team by [insert your specific reason and use the pitch we built in the Sell Yourself chapter]."

Then add why you want to be at their school specifically, not just because of football. That is what can get coaches over the fence because they know you won't just use them and leave. If you are serious about a major there, the location, family ties, or a school program, tell them. That kind of detail shows you are not just looking for any offer. You are looking for the right one, and that makes coaches more willing to invest their time in you.

Template:

I also want to be here because (insert personal reason: major, location, family connection, etc.). This isn't just a football decision for me. I believe this is the right fit on and off the field."

Here is an example of a pitch that turned into an offer:

"Coach, I've done my homework on your program and your system. I know you run a 4-2-5 and rotate your edge rushers often. I've studied the film from this season, and I see a clear gap in setting the edge on short-yardage plays. That's what I do best. I believe I can help your team win in those situations."

I also want to be here because you offer a Sports Medicine program, and that's what I want to study. This isn't just about football. I believe this is the right fit for my future too."

Then depending on where things go, you can ask questions like:

- *"Are you currently recruiting my position for the [Grad Year] class?"*
- *"What does the process usually look like from here?"*
- *"Would you be open to sharing this with the [Position Coach For Your Position]?"*

This is where you shift from highlight tape to real conversation. Show them you're a serious student of the game and committed to earning your spot, not just another hopeful recruit.

• • •

E = Elevate the Moment

If they start sharing your video up the coaching chain, stay calm, be patient, and be ready to deliver your pitch again. If an offer comes in the room, that's great, follow the post-offer steps from the Ask for the Offer chapter. But if it doesn't, don't leave empty-handed.

Ask for their cell phone number and the best time to follow up.

Confirm your next play:

"Would it be alright if I check back with you next week?" or

"What is your cell phone number?"

Your question will depend on where you leave off. Send a handwritten thank-you note by mail. Mention something specific you talked about and thank them for their time.

Template:

Coach [Last Name],

Thank you for taking the time to meet with me the other day. It meant a lot, especially since I walked in unannounced.

I really appreciated the chance to share my film with you and talk about how I could potentially contribute to your program. What stood out to me most was [insert example of something important they said].

(School name) is my dream school, and I'm willing to work and earn everything.

Thank you again for your time and I look forward to speaking again soon.

(Your First & Last Name)

(Link To Your Highlight Video)

This is what separates the kids who walk in with confidence from the ones who wait around hoping for a call. If you do this right, you'll stand out. Not just because of your film.

Because you had the guts to show up, prepared and professional, when 99% of kids never will.

Narci's story is just one example of many athletes I've mentored using this exact strategy, who have seen similar or even the same results.

It's extremely rare for a player to follow this entire playbook and the FACE Play™ and walk away with nothing. But it only works when the fit is right and the preparation is locked in. Walking in the front door works. Most players will never take that step. But the ones who do? They stand out. And they get results.

KEY TAKEAWAYS

- A lack of response doesn't always mean no. It means it's time to get more aggressive.
- When all else fails, walking in the front door is a great next play.
- Every detail matters: donuts, dress, handshake, eye contact, pitch. They either build your credibility or hurt it.
- You only get one shot when a coach hits play. If your highlight video isn't ready and dialed in, it's game over. Make sure to get an evaluation and confirm you're targeting a school that can offer you.
- The best pitch is simple, confident, and focused on the program's needs, not yours.
- Coaches don't just offer based on talent. They offer based on confidence, initiative, and professionalism. Narci brought all three of those other attributes.

YOUR NEXT PLAY

- If there is a school you really want to speak with from your Big Board, but no offer, then consider executing this strategy.
- Make sure your son is professionally evaluated and that the school is truly the right fit. (Get a professional evaluation at Gonextplay.com/evaluation)

- Follow the FACE Play™ to the letter.
- Send a handwritten thank-you note. Lock in your follow-up. Track the result. And then move to the next school on the list.

PLAY 15: THE NEXT PLAY RULE

"There is no failure…only your Next Play"

RICHIE CONTARTESI

I've said it before, but it bears repeating. After my parents got divorced and I failed 5th grade, I felt broken. It wasn't just a rough year. I truly believed something was wrong with me. I had no confidence. I couldn't focus on school. I didn't want to talk to anyone. I didn't even want to be around people. I just wanted to disappear.

The only thing that gave me any kind of hope was football. Football was the one place I felt alive. The field was the only space where I could breathe. I was sitting in my bedroom, staring at the University of Miami football requirements. I had printed them out and taped them to my wall. I had no idea how I'd ever get there, but that piece of paper was the only dream I had left.

Even though my life felt like it was falling apart, I kept looking at that sheet like maybe, just maybe, there was still a way forward. However, I played wide receiver, and I had one big problem…

I couldn't catch the ball.

I tried everything. New gloves. New cleats. I got to practice early. I stayed late. But none of it worked. Every time the quarterback threw the ball my way, my heart would start racing. And the second the ball was in the air, I panicked. I couldn't help it. My mind would race back to the last pass I dropped. Or I'd start thinking about what my dad might say if I dropped another one.

Or worse, what if I actually caught it and didn't know what to do next? And one day at practice, it happened again. A perfect spiral came straight to me. I reached up to grab it, and boom. It bounced right off my chest. Right then, I saw Coach Mike Jalad walking over to me.

Coach Jalad never yelled, but he was the kind of coach you didn't want to disappoint. When he walked toward you, you paid attention. I braced myself for him to get on me. I knew I deserved it. But he didn't. He just looked me in the eye and asked one question:

"Richie… what are you thinking about when the ball's in the air?"

That question hit me like a truck. I froze for a second in deep thought. Then I told him the truth. "I guess, I'm thinking about the last pass I dropped. Or what my dad's going to say. Or maybe what happens if I actually catch it and mess it up after."

He nodded and looked at me. "I see you working harder than everyone. You've got new gloves. New cleats. First one here to practice everyday. Last one to leave. But until you focus on the ball in front of you, you're never going to catch it."

Then he asked me a question that changed my life. "Richie, what's the most important play?"

I shrugged, frustrated. "I don't know." He nudged me. "Come on. What's the most important play?"

Finally, he said, "The next play?"

Then he asked me three more questions. Back to back. "What are you going to do differently this time?"

I said, "I'll catch it with my hands."

He said, "How are you going to do that?"

"I guess I'll put my hands out like this," I said, showing him my form.

He grabbed my hands and adjusted them slightly. "No, like this. Good. Now, when are you going to do that?"

I said, "Next time the ball's in the air." He nodded. "Good. Let's go. Back in the huddle."

As I jogged back to the huddle, something clicked. Maybe the last drop didn't matter. Maybe the mistake I made before wasn't the end. Maybe everything I'd done wrong, all the pain I'd carried, all the failure I felt, maybe none of it had to define me. All that mattered now was what I did next.

From that moment on, my focus changed. I stopped thinking about the past. I stopped stressing over the future. I locked in on the next play.

But it didn't just help me. After that day, Coach Jalad started using the Next Play motto with everyone on the team. And at the time, we were 0–4. We weren't a very good team. We made a lot of mistakes. Guys were getting frustrated. Some were giving up. But that's when everything changed.

Anytime someone messed up in practice or during a game, he'd walk over, and say, "Hey! What's the most important play?" And all of us would yell back, "Next play!"

And it wasn't just for the mistakes. If someone made a great play but celebrated too long, he'd say the same thing. "What's the most important play?"

"Next play!"

We said it so often that it became our identity. And once it became our identity, everything changed. We didn't just start playing better. We started winning. We ended that season as champions.

Coach Jalad taught me something bigger than just how to move on from a bad play. He taught me how to create a culture. A culture where there is no failure. Only your Next Play.

And it wasn't just a mindset. It became a rule I followed anytime I felt down, frustrated, or stuck. A rule I could hand to others when they were ready to give up. A rule made up of just three questions:

1. What?
2. How?
3. When?

That's it. And this rule works because the real cause of being stuck isn't just failure. It's not knowing what to do next. That's where depression comes from. And in the recruiting process, that's where athletes lose confidence. That's where parents feel helpless.

FINDING FOCUS

Any time I felt stuck, I would say "Next Play" and immediately answer three questions. That simple reset helped me stop spiraling and start moving forward. It gave me a way to refocus, take control, and act with clarity instead of emotion.

Before, I used to overthink everything. I would get in my head, dwell on mistakes, and lose confidence. But once I had this rule, I stopped feeling stuck. I always knew what to do next, and I executed. I was focused.

And when I started using it with my teammates, it helped them too. It gave all of us a way to turn mistakes into a learning experience. A way to stay focused, take ownership, and keep moving forward.

That's exactly what this rule does for athletes. It creates focus. And focus is everything. Because without it, even the most talented athletes fail and never get back up.

But with it? They take action. They build momentum. They keep improving. And they don't quit.

Focus is what separates the kids who fall off after a few rejections from the ones who get offers. It's what keeps your son moving forward while everyone else freezes. That's why this rule matters. Because it gives him the power to focus on one thing. His Next Play.

There's a famous story about Warren Buffett and Bill Gates. They were at a dinner party together, and someone asked them to each write down the one word that best explained their success.

They both wrote down the same word, focus.

If two of the most successful people in the world agree that focus is the key, then the real question is, how do we create it for your son?

This rule is how. It shifts your focus away from fear, the past, the future, or worry, and brings it back to your Next Play.

But it's not just about being focused. It's about being focused on the right things.

Most people go their whole lives focusing on the wrong things. They dwell on the past. They worry about the future. They care too much about what other people think.

And when that becomes a habit, it leads to excuses, procrastination, blaming others, and self-doubt.

I'm not saying your son is someone who makes excuses. But maybe he's developed a habit of having reasons why it's not working.

I'm not saying your son is a procrastinator. He might just have a habit of pushing things off.

I'm not saying your son doesn't take responsibility. But maybe he just has a habit of blaming others.

And I'm not saying your son doesn't believe in himself. But maybe the real problem is that he has a bad habit of self-doubt.

The truth is, when you focus on your Next Play, you enter a state of flow which was first studied by psychologist Mihaly Csikszentmihalyi, who wrote the book *Flow*, which I highly recommend reading.

Flow is an optimal state of consciousness. It's where you feel and perform your absolute best. When your son is fully locked in. On the field. In the weight room. On the phone with a coach. Time either flies or slows down, and everything just clicks.

I'll never forget my junior year. It was the fourth quarter with under two minutes to go. We were down by six. Our school had never won a football game in its entire history.

I lined up at slot receiver. The play was a post route. I took off and as I turned my head, I saw the quarterback rolling out. He planted his feet and launched the ball. And as that ball floated through the air, time slowed down.

It felt like it was in the air forever. I tracked it. I caught it. Touchdown. We won the first game in school history. That's flow.

Or think about when you're at the office. You're locked in. Fully focused. And the next thing you know, you look at the clock and it's 5 p.m. That's flow too.

And when you stay focused on your Next Play, you create that kind of flow more often.

Why does that matter? Because flow isn't just a good feeling. It boosts performance.

McKinsey & Company studied over 10,000 high-performing executives. They found that when someone enters a state of flow, their productivity increases by up to 500 percent.

That's five times more messages sent, coaches talked with, visits, and offers.

So whether your son is on the field, in the weight room, or handling the business side of recruiting, when he's in that state of flow, he'll show up at his best.

And it all starts by focusing on one thing, your Next Play.

In football, choosing your Next Play is simple. You drop a pass, you fix your hands. You miss a tackle, you lift your head. The play is clear. But in business and in sales, it's not that simple.

I quickly realized that the rule alone wasn't enough. I thought just having a Next Play was all anyone needed because it worked so well on the football field. But I was wrong.

Whether I got fired from my first job or struggled to get traction in business, I learned the hard way that just saying "Next Play" and picking any play wasn't going to work.

Some athletes, and even my team members, despite having the same playbook, the same tools, and the same coaching, still struggled to execute consistently.

PUTTING ADVICE INTO PRACTICE

When I was building my business, I started hiring employees. I started building a sales team. These were great people who were smart, driven, and talented. But they were either guessing their Next Play based on how they felt or not following through executing it.

My mentor said that I needed to coach them every week. So I started coaching them the same way Coach Jalad coached me. Each week, I'd sit down with them one on one. First, we'd review their wins. Then I'd ask, "What's your next play?"

At first, that helped. It gave them direction. But over time, I noticed we weren't always moving in the right direction. They weren't improving. They weren't focused on the most important activities. We were guessing and the plays we were choosing weren't actually solving the real problems we were facing.

I called my mentor and told him it wasn't working. He asked me how I was helping my team choose their Next Play.

I told him that I would ask them what they thought, and they'd say things like, "I feel like XYZ is happening," or "I think it's probably XYZ."

And he said, "That's the problem."

He told me, "You can't just guess and pick your Next Play based on what you think or how you feel. You have to use data. You have to find the real bottleneck. What's holding them back right now? Where's the actual challenge?"

And he was right. The only way to find that is by tracking your KPIs (Key Performance Indicators).

So of course, we still kept reviewing the wins. But instead of jumping straight to the next play like before, we added something new. We looked at the KPIs like calls made, connects made, calls booked, outreach completed, and more.

After making the change, the ones who were improving the fastest weren't just doing more. They were improving in the right areas. Once we found the real problem, the real reason someone was stuck or not performing as well as they could be, I could help them choose the right next play to fix it.

Like if someone was sending emails but not getting any responses, we could now look at the data. And let's say the open rate was really low. Before, we wouldn't have known that was the issue so we might've changed the content of the email itself. But the real problem wasn't what they were saying. It was the subject line.

Because we reviewed all the data, we could now adjust or improve the right things at the right time. But even after choosing the right plays, it still didn't always get done, especially as my team grew.

So it all came down to the last most important part of the entire system, accountability. The fact that I met with them every single week meant they knew I was going to review the numbers. I was going to ask, "Did you do your play from last week?" There were no excuses. Just honesty, because the data doesn't lie.

It was about helping each person on my team become the best they could possibly be. I wasn't there to micromanage. I was there to coach. And they wanted to be coached. They were hungry. They just needed coaching, a clear next play, and someone who cared enough to hold them accountable.

I didn't realize it at the time, but what Coach Jalad taught me back then, the way he shifted our focus after every win or loss, is the same thing I was doing now in business.

He didn't just help us win games. He created a culture where we didn't dwell on the past or get distracted by the future. He eliminated failure. Because there was no failure, and only ever one thing to focus on—the next play.

I'll never forget the day it all came together. I had just heard that one of our team members had a really rough call. I walked into our team meeting, looked around the room, and said, "There is no failure…only your Next Play."

Then I looked at her and asked, "What's your Next Play?"

She answered without hesitation, her what, her how, and her when.

That moment hit different. It wasn't just a quote. It became our standard. Everyone else in the room leaned in and said, "Let's go."

And not only did she get motivated and get back to work, but so did everyone else. It became how we operated. It became how we showed up every single day.

Now we have that quote printed on the wall in our office. Because it's not just a saying. It's how you win. Coach Jalad instilled the Next Play® in me. My parents and mentors doubled down on it. And over time, I built a system around it.

The result in my life? I kept going. For example, I wrote a book that eventually became an Amazon #1 best seller. But I would never have imagined when I was failing fifth grade (because I struggled to focus in order to read and write) that I'd write *anything* worth reading, let alone a book. Yet years later, despite doubting every word, rewriting entire chapters, and leaning on my dad to guide me, I sat down and wrote one anyway.

I also pushed through 10 years of failure in business. I tried everything. Partners quit on me. I lost money. I lost confidence. I thought about quitting more times than I can count. But I didn't. I kept showing up. And eventually, I built a successful one.

And in football, I wasn't the biggest or the fastest. I got overlooked. I got cut. I sat on the bench. But I kept working. I kept showing up. And I earned a full-ride Division 1 scholarship to Ole Miss. I got to run out of the tunnel at schools like Alabama and LSU. I made SEC catches in front of 100,000 people at Tennessee and 90,000 at Arkansas. Not because I was the most talented, but because I never stopped focusing on my next play.

And at the Next Play HQ, we created a culture where everyone on my team is held accountable to achieving their dream in life and always focused on their Next Play. A culture built on moving forward, getting better, and never giving up.

HELPING OTHERS

Most importantly, I gained the ability to help other people do the same kind of thing. It would mean nothing if it only helped me or just my team members. But now, like Coach Jalad helped me, I get to help others all over the world live their dreams too.

The Next Play® Accountability System changed everything, not just in my business and life, but in how I lead and coach others. In fact, leaders from other companies across the country started noticing and asking how I did it. That's when I began consulting with sales teams at organizations like IBM, HP, and NRG Energy.

Everyone claims they want accountability. In business. In sports. From their team. But when it comes down to actually implementing this principle, most people don't follow through because they have no process to turn to. No system. Just the same words, "Be accountable."And by itself, that means nothing.

The problem is, most people only hold others accountable to the past. What they said they were going to do. And while that matters, what's even more powerful is holding someone accountable to their Next Play. And even more than that? Holding them accountable to their dream. To their commitment.

And while companies were paying me from $35,000 to $150,000 to teach this system to corporate teams, neither the money nor the context got me excited. I wasn't nearly as passionate about helping executives in boardrooms as I was about coaching young men—who were just like me—to run out of the tunnel on Saturdays.

But I'm grateful for that experience. Because it taught me how to build an accountability system that actually works. How to coach people. And how to hold them accountable in a way that creates results.

So when I started mentoring high school football players full-time, I already had the playbook. I realized that the same things that held back my corporate clients and sales professionals were holding back young athletes too.

These young men, ages 14 to 18, are running a business. They're selling themselves. They're marketing themselves. They're building relationships and managing rejection.

And just like adults, they didn't want more hype. They wanted coaching. They wanted mentorship. They wanted accountability. They wanted a system that actually worked.

They wanted someone to believe in them and push them to a higher standard, not just in football, but in life. That's when I knew this system would be critical to their success.

Because you can't just tell young men to be accountable. They have to take ownership. But even the most responsible young men still need a plan.

They need to be coached and held accountable, not just to what they said they were going to do, but to achieving what they committed to and who they committed to becoming.

From the very first chapter of this book, when your son signed his commitment, that became the anchor. Whenever I start working with an athlete and he sends a picture of his signed commitment, I know I can mentor him. I can coach him. And I can hold him accountable to achieving that dream.

No one wants to be held accountable to failure. But the reason this system works is because we don't guess. We find the actual problem. We coach each athlete through the right Next Play. And we hold them accountable. Not just to the past. Not just to their next play. But to the commitment they made on day one.

Today, I use this exact system I'm sharing below with every athlete we mentor and now I want to give it to you. In this chapter, I'm going to walk you through the full Next Play® Accountability System.

It's the same system we use every week to keep athletes unstuck, focused, and executing regardless of fear, failure, rejection, or setbacks.

No more talk about motivation and accountability, because this isn't talk. It's a proven system. Built from real struggle, real coaching, and real results. Motivation fades, but accountability wins.

Almost every parent I speak with before we meet initially believes that if their son just knows what to do, he'll succeed. That's what I used to believe too. It seems obvious. Give them the plan. Show them the steps. Walk through the plays. And they'll follow through. Right?

But after working with hundreds of athletes, I quickly realized that knowing what to do isn't the real problem. Most of these athletes are already high achievers. They're responsible. They have great GPAs, and they're already successful in school.

Your son could have all the information. He could know exactly what to say, how to say it, and when to say it. But without the right game plan, without a properly structured highlight video, without targeting the right schools based on his true level, without consistent coaching to improve his marketing and sales, and without accountability to stay focused and take action every week, your son will not get the best results possible.

Sure, he might get an offer here or there. But is that really what your son is after? Is that the vision he wrote down in the commitment he signed?

That's why this chapter is so critical. Whether you work with a mentor like me or choose to guide your son yourself, without this system in place, he will struggle.

That's the real reason most athletes fail in recruiting. Not because they aren't talented. Not because they don't care. Not because they couldn't just read this book or watch my YouTube videos and learn what to post on social media.

They fail because no one coached them through every step. No one kept them focused on their Next Play after being rejected over and over. No one showed them what to do when things got hard. And no one held them accountable to their dream like my mentors did for me.

But why is that? Players have coaches on the field. So why don't they have coaches for the business side of recruiting? I ask that question every single day because it's what I wish I had. And it's why I do what I do today.

We expect 14 to 18-year-olds to be expert marketers and salespeople with zero coaching. That makes no sense. That's why I'm on a mission to make business coaching for athletes the new norm.

Because when they get ghosted, they spiral. When a coach says no, they feel like it's over. When another player commits, they start believing they're too late. And that's when they stop taking action or never start at all.

That's not a recruiting problem. That's a focus and follow-through problem. And it doesn't mean your son is lazy or not built for this. It just means he's never had a system to stay focused. A system to stay confident. A system that shows him how to keep moving forward no matter what happens.

Most athletes don't need more information. They don't need more motivation. What they really need is coaching and accountability. That's what the Next Play® Accountability System provides.

NEXT PLAY® ACCOUNTABILITY SYSTEM

It's a simple, step-by-step system made up of five clear steps:

1. Step 1: Submit the Scorecard
   - Ownership starts here. Your son reflects on his week and submits his data.
2. Step 2: Celebrate the Wins
   - Start with progress. Build belief. Anchor to momentum before fixing anything.
3. Step 3: Review the KPIs
   - Dig into the data. Don't guess. Use facts to find the real constraint.
4. Step 4: Choose the Next Play
   - One action. One focus. Defined by three questions: What?, How?, and When?
5. Step 5: Hold Him Accountable
   - Review the past. Reinforce the Next Play. Reconnect to the dream.

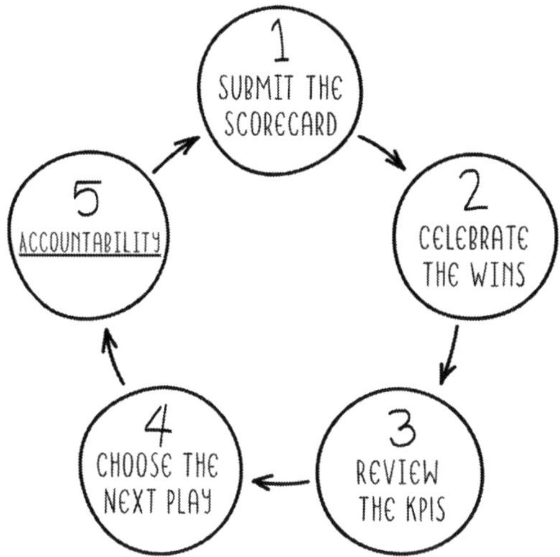

Step 1 - Submit your Scorecard

Every week starts with a scorecard submission. Your son fills out a scorecard that includes:

- His biggest wins from the week
- His key performance indicators (KPIs)
- His current Next Play (what?, how?, and when?)

But this step is not just about filling out a form. It's about building awareness, discipline, and ownership. Most athletes never stop to track or reflect. The scorecard forces clarity. And once your son starts doing it, everything changes because he actually starts working on his business, not just in it.

Most business owners stay stuck on a hamster wheel because they only focus on doing the work. But the moment you step back, look at the data, and measure your progress, you gain something more powerful. You gain perspective and that's what the scorecard gives your son.

What gets measured gets improved. Tracking weekly activity is one of the fastest ways to find problems early and take action to solve them. Just like a coach watches film and tracks stats, this scorecard does the same thing, but for recruiting.

And even though it looks long, the scorecard usually only takes about five minutes to fill out. Why? Because our athletes track everything inside the Next Play CRM each day. This is why I highly suggest using a CRM. By the end of the week, it's all there. All they have to do is review their numbers, reflect, and submit.

- Did you execute your play from last week?
- What are your wins for the week?
- How many questionnaires did you fill out?
- How many emails did you send to college coaches?
- How many DMs did you send to college coaches?
- How many responses did you get from coaches?
- How many cold calls did you make? (optional)
- How many cold call connects did you have? (optional)
- How many days did you post on social media?
- How many calls did you book with college coaches?
- How many coaches showed up to those calls?
- How many visit invites did you get?
- How many visits did you go on?
- How many offers did you receive?

This level of tracking separates average athletes from scholarship athletes. If your son can't measure his activity, he can't improve it.

Step 2 - Celebrate the Wins

Now that you have the data, you can begin your weekly 1-on-1 Next Play Sessions with your son. Set aside 20 minutes each week to sit down with him, and always start with something positive.

Before fixing anything or digging into numbers, celebrate the wins. Whether it is a coach's response, a booked visit, more outreach than last week, or just added confidence on a call, start there.

This might sound small, but it's critical. Most athletes spend all week chasing results. They focus so much on what's not working that they miss how much they're actually growing.

In the Next Play system, this is exactly how we do it. Every week we meet 1-on-1 with each athlete, and we always celebrate wins first. We show him that progress is happening. He's improving. He's putting in the work. And even if the results aren't there yet, he can see that he's moving in the right direction.

This is how we build belief. This is how we fuel confidence. Because when an athlete believes they're improving, they stay motivated. They take more action. They push through the hard weeks. And that's what leads to results.

So we never skip this step. Wins come first.

Step 3 - Review the KPIs

This is where things get fun. After celebrating the wins, we dive into the numbers. Or, as I like to call them, the facts. Just like film doesn't lie, neither does the data. We look at the scorecard and ask, "Where is your son stuck right now?"

We're not guessing. We're not relying on how he feels or what he thinks. We're using facts to find the most important constraint.

And yes, you might find more than one challenge. But the real question is, which one matters most? Which challenge, if solved or adjusted, would move the needle the most? That is the one we want to attack first.

The bulk of these were shared in earlier chapters, but let's break it down with a few examples:

- If your son is sending emails but getting no responses, we check the open rate.
    - If the open rate is low, the subject line probably isn't grabbing attention. We coach him to test better subject lines or send at better times of day.
    - If the open rate is high, but no one replies, the message itself likely needs to be more personalized or clearer. So we fix that.

- If coaches are replying but not booking calls, we look at the call-to-action.
    - Is your son actually asking to schedule a call? We teach him how to use clear, confident language that moves the conversation forward.
    - Is his highlight tape positioned right? Maybe the order is wrong, or the plays aren't set up properly.
    - Is he targeting the right level? If he's chasing Power Five schools but playing at a Division 2 level, we need to realign his list.

- If calls are booked but no visits follow, we coach him on how to lead the conversation.
    - Is he asking the right questions?
    - Is he building a real connection?
    - Is he selling himself like someone a coach wants on campus?

- If there's interest but no offers, we ask:
  - Is he asking the right question at the right time? If he isn't asking what it takes to earn an offer, or is asking that question too early, it can stall the process.
  - Is he proving his value clearly enough? Coaches might be interested but still unsure if he can compete and contribute at their level.

When you track KPIs the right way, the real problem becomes obvious. But choosing which problem to solve first is where experience comes in.

The truth is, there are thousands of possible variables, constraints, and solutions. But as you repeat this process each week, you'll get better and better at identifying the most important challenge to fix. That's what makes this system so powerful.

Here are the KPI targets for the players I mentor. For every 60 area coaches found:

- 40 coaches should watch his highlight video (67% conversion)
- 15 recruiting calls should be booked from those views (25% conversion)
- 7 official visit invitations should come from those calls (12% conversion)
- 3 scholarship offers should result from those visits (5% conversion)

	AREA COACHES	VIDEO VIEWS	VIEW %	CALLS BOOKED	CALL %
	60	40	67%	15	25%
	60	45	75%	18	30%
	60	35	58%	12	20%

	CALLS BOOKED	VISITS BOOKED	VISIT %	OFFERS MADE	OFFER %
	15	9	15%	4	7%
	15	6	10%	2	3%
	15	4	7%	1	2%

These are not random numbers. They're proven benchmarks based on hundreds of successful athletes we've coached. They give your son something concrete to aim for and show you exactly where he stands each week.

This step turns recruiting from a guessing game into a coaching process. It's how we solve the real problem instead of wasting time fixing the wrong things.

Step 4 - Prescribe the Next Play

Now that we've identified the real challenge using data, it's time to choose the Next Play. This is the hardest part of the process. Pick the right play, and your son's recruiting can take a huge leap forward. Keep choosing the wrong plays, and he could miss out on the offers he's worked so hard for.

This is where the Next Play® Rule comes in. Your son can use it any time he feels stuck or unsure what to do next. But it's also the anchor of our weekly accountability sessions. It gives him one clear focus every single week.

Identifying the challenge through KPIs is hard. But choosing the right Next Play to solve it? That's even harder. And that's where real coaching makes all the difference. One wrong play can waste a week. Doing too much can lead to a feeling of being overwhelmed. Good coaches do two things:

- They help the athlete find the most important constraint right now.
- They help him choose one clear, focused play to solve it.

But the great coaches? They do both and guide the athlete to choose it himself.

Because when your son takes ownership, when he says, "Here's my play, here's how I'll do it, and here's when I'll do it," he will do it. That's when the process becomes his. And when it becomes his, he not only does it, but the results follow.

We coach each athlete to answer three simple questions:

- What is the play?
  - (Example: Send a follow-up message to 10 schools.)

- How will he do it?
  - (Example: Use a stronger subject line and a better customized intro paragraph using the bios this time.)

- When will he do it?
  - (Example: Every evening for one hour after practice this week.

This removes guesswork and emotion. He's no longer reacting to rejection. He's taking clear action with focus and purpose. Most importantly, he's learning how to lead himself.

Recruiting setbacks like being ghosted by a coach or having a visit fall through are not failures. They are just feedback. They reveal what needs to improve.

And instead of spiraling, your son stays locked in on what's next. Here are a few examples:

- A coach didn't respond? → He updates the message and follows up.
- A recruiting call went badly? → He roleplays the next one and gets better.
- No invite after a great conversation? → He reviews how he asked and sharpens the ask.

That's how your son gets better. Not with a magic pill. Not with motivation. But by choosing the right Next Play and executing, one play at a time.

Step 5 - Hold Him Accountable

We meet with every athlete we mentor once a week. We call these Next Play Sessions. And they are the heartbeat of this system. These meetings are short, usually no longer than 20 minutes. But the impact is massive.

Every week, we repeat the same process. Not just when motivation strikes. Not just when things are going well or falling apart. Every single week. Why? Because we're talking about 14 to 18-year-old young men, who are easily distracted. And because this is what creates consistency.

Weekly 1-on-1 Next Play Sessions allow your son to step back, review the data, identify what's working, and make smarter decisions. They help him work on his business, not just in it.

Each week, you'll check to confirm whether your son followed through on the play from the week before. You don't just hope he followed through. You review the scorecard. You ask the hard questions. And you measure the result.

- Did he do his play?
- Did he do it well?
- Did he improve from last week?

This is not about being perfect. It's about showing up, being honest, and doing what he said he was going to do. This is not micromanagement. It's championship-level standards. The same way a football coach watches film and reviews every rep, you're reviewing your son's reps in the recruiting process.

Because recruiting is a business. And if no one's reviewing the film, he's just guessing. But it's also about looking forward. You don't just ask, "Did you do your play?" You remind him what he's committed to. You connect his Next Play back to the dream he wrote down in Chapter 1. That commitment is the anchor.

So even if he has a rough week, even if things don't go as planned, you don't let him spiral. You bring him back to the dream. Back to the vision. Back to the commitment.

That's why this works so well. Because the accountability isn't just to a task or to the past. It's to doing whatever it takes to achieve the dream. It's to who he said he wanted to become.

And it's not just about outreach and marketing either. You can hold your son accountable in every part of the process:

- Highlight video optimization – Is it updated? Is it level-matched? Is it improving?
- Position-specific skill development – Is he working on the areas college coaches care most about?
- Game performance – Is he putting the right plays on film every Friday?

Recruiting is both product and business. The product is your son's ability and performance. The business is how he markets and sells himself to coaches. Both must be coached. Both must be reviewed.

One of our athletes, Wyatt Rinderer, started with an NAIA evaluation. After making specific adjustments to his highlight film based on what college coaches at the next level needed to see, he jumped to Division 2.

Now, he's aiming for Division 1 FCS. That didn't happen by accident. It happened because he developed the right position-specific skills, took action one play at a time, added what was missing to his game film the next season, and stayed accountable every single week.

That's the power of Next Play® accountability. On the field. In the film room. And in the business of recruiting.

KEY TAKEAWAYS

- There is no failure. Only your Next Play. That's the mindset. No matter what happened last week, what matters most is what your son chooses to do next.
- Focus is everything. When your son has one clear action to take each week, he stops overthinking, starts executing, and builds real momentum.
- The Next Play® Rule is how he resets. Anytime he feels stuck, frustrated, or overwhelmed, he answers three simple questions: What? How? When?
- Most athletes don't fail because they aren't good enough. They fail because they don't have a coach helping them to stay focused, to solve the right problems, and to keep showing up after things go wrong.
- The Next Play® Accountability System changes that. It gives your son a structure to follow every week. A process to build discipline, confidence, and results—one play at a time.
- Tracking KPIs, diagnosing the real constraint, and choosing the right play is what separates scholarship athletes from everyone else. It's not just about effort. It's about effort applied to the right things.
- This isn't a motivational speech. It's a proven system. When executed every week, it leads to real growth, real improvement, and real offers.

YOUR NEXT PLAY

- Download our weekly scorecard template and weekly 1-on-1 Next Play Session tracking spreadsheet for free at GoNextPlay.com/resources.

- Start the Scorecard habit this week. Set a specific day and time to sit down with your son. Have him track and submit his activity using the questions in this chapter.
- Lead a 20-minute weekly 1-on-1 Next Play Session. Use the five-step process.
- Print his signed commitment and have it readily available during each session.
- Repeat this process every week.

WIN THE GAME

THE RESULT

"What you get by achieving your goals is not as important as who you become in the process."

ZIG ZIGLAR

It was a Tuesday evening when my phone rang. It was Chris.

A few months earlier, Chris had come to me like so many other players do—a solid football player with a big dream, but no offers or plan. From day one, I could tell he wasn't the loudest kid in the room, but there was something about him. He was different. I could tell whether it was football or something else, he was going to be successful.

In the beginning, when I gave Chris an assignment, he didn't push it off or make excuses. He executed. He built his Big Board. He learned how to pitch himself. He posted consistently on social media. He reached out to coaches every single week.

And it worked. Chris went from being an unknown name to landing calls, generating lots of interest, and even earning his first scholarship offer. He was doing everything right. But then, all of a sudden, things slowed down.

I checked the Next Play CRM and saw he wasn't taking action like he had in the beginning. So when I saw his name pop up on my phone that night, I knew something was going on.

In a slight worry, I picked up.

"Coach Richie," he said. "I need to talk to you about something." His voice sounded different, missing the excited, nervous energy I'd heard before.

"Go for it," I said.

He took a breath. "I love football. But…I think I've found something I love even more."

I paused, waiting.

"I started detailing cars in my neighborhood," he said. "At first, it was just a way to make some cash. But then I started doing what you taught me for recruiting, marketing myself, confidently communicating, selling myself, using a CRM, and following up. I made a website for it. I knocked on doors. I treated every car like it belonged to an NFL coach."

He chuckled. "And now…it's blowing up. I've got more customers than I can keep up with. I'm making more than I can imagine and I'm getting ready to start hiring and expanding."

There was a long pause. Then he said it.

"Coach Richie…I know we've worked so hard for these offers, but I want to keep growing my business full-time. I've realized I really enjoy the game of business."

At first, it stung a little. This decision meant Chris wasn't going to play college football. But I wasn't disappointed.

Because in that moment, I realized something. Chris hadn't just learned how to play the recruiting game. He had learned how to play the game of business.

And the confidence to go after what he wants. Not just what you learn from reading a business book or taking a business course. But the kind that comes from being taught, coached to execute it the right way, and held accountable every step of the way.

When you first picked up this book, you probably thought it was just about earning offers. And yes, 89% of the athletes I mentor who follow it earn football scholarships. But you might be wondering, what about the other 11%?

Well, they decided to choose another path. They made it clear to me that it was 100% worth the time, nothing was wasted, and they're proud they went after their dream with two feet, all in.

In fact, most parents who reach out to me tell me that the scholarship wasn't even the result they cared about most.

The real result?

It's watching their son grow into a young man who knows how to set a vision, commit to something far outside his comfort zone, create a game plan, execute it without fear, and build the confidence to chase big opportunities on and off the field.

It's seeing him develop the kind of skills that will serve him for the rest of his life. The ability to overcome fear, push through rejection, and stop worrying about what people think.

Skills like:

- Business skills

- Marketing skills
- Communication skills
- Sales skills
- Leadership Skills

Skills that could lead to starting his own business like Chris, working his way up the corporate ladder, landing job offers, confidently leading a team at work, earning promotions, building strong relationships, and yes, even getting the girl of his dreams.

These aren't just football skills. They're life skills, because at the end of the day not everyone is going to get the $100M NFL contract. Chris's story proved to me that this process is about so much more than football.

Yes, the vision may be earning a scholarship. But the real result, the thing that changes your son's future, is learning to commit to a process far outside his comfort zone, to stay accountable, and to push through fear and adversity.

This playbook teaches your son how to do that. In Chapter 1, I told you there are 1.1 million high school football players in America. And only 2% will ever earn a football scholarship. That's the reality. But I also told you something else.

When athletes follow this playbook exactly, 100% of them have earned scholarships.

But even if your son chooses a different life path—like Chris did— he'll walk away with something even more valuable than a football scholarship: confidence.

Confidence in himself. Confidence in his ability to build something from nothing. Confidence to take a dream, create a plan, and execute it relentlessly without fear, no matter what.

Confidence to go after anything he wants in his life and believe in himself because he knows no matter what happens and what adversity he faces, he will overcome it.

Whether he earns a football scholarship, builds a business like Chris, or chases another dream entirely, these skills will carry him for the rest of his life.

When he learns to market himself, communicate with confidence, and ask for what he's earned, when he focuses on his Next Play no matter what, he won't just become a scholarship athlete.

He'll become a confident young man who knows how to win.

That's the real result, and that's my hope for your family. Maybe that's why Chris's story hits me so hard.

Because I remember being that kid. 5'7", 150 pounds, sprinting to the travel squad list every Thursday at Ole Miss. I know what it feels like to want something so badly that it keeps you up at night, but not having the confidence off the field to pursue it.

I also know what it feels like to have someone believe in you enough to keep you focused on your Next Play when you're ready to quit. Having someone in your corner who believes in you and helps you build these skills.

It's the only reason I was able to write this book. I never thought, "I can't do this." I didn't procrastinate. The day I decided to write it, I just did.

It's the same with building my business, Next Play. After I saw the impact I had on the first player I mentored, I realized this was what I was meant to do with my life, and just like with this book, I didn't hesitate. I just built it.

And it's the same with anything I take on now. Why?

Because I had to overcome something that challenged me beyond anything I imagined. And I'm not talking about the usual challenges in school or sports that every kid faces. I'm talking about what happens when young men follow this playbook and push themselves far outside their comfort zone. When they discover who they really are and what they're capable of.

Today, I believe deep down that I can do anything. And that is exactly what I want for your son, for him to wake up every day knowing he has what it takes, no matter what life throws at him to pursue his dreams.

That's my mission. To make young men confident again. That's why I wrote this book.

Not just so your son can play football, but so he can build the kind of confidence that will allow him to achieve whatever he wants in life.

No more waiting for the perfect time. No more worrying about what others think. No more hesitating.

Now it's time for your son to commit to the process, take ownership of his success, and focus on his Next Play.

And when he does, eventually, he'll get the result.

I'd Love To Hear From You

Thank you so much for reading this book-it means the world to me. If you found it helpful, inspiring, or just enjoyable, would you take a moment to leave a review?

Your feedback not only helps others but also keeps me motivated to create more valuable content for you.

Here's how you can leave a review:

1. Scan the QR code on this page to go directly to the review page.
2. Or, visit your Amazon Orders page, find this book, and click "Write a Product Review."

Your kind words make a big difference. Thank you for your support!

The Scholarship Legacy Log

After you earn your scholarship, we'd love for you to pass this book down to another teammate chasing the same dream. Just like libraries in the old days, sign your name here to mark your place in this book's history.

Instructions:

1. Write your name, graduating class, position, and phone number.
2. Leave a short message or piece of advice for the next athlete.
3. Pass the book forward.

Name:	
Graduating Class:	
Position:	
Phone Number:	
Message to the Next Athlete:	

Name:	
Graduating Class:	
Position:	
Phone Number:	
Message to the Next Athlete:	

Name:	
Graduating Class:	
Position:	
Phone Number:	
Message to the Next Athlete:	

Name:	
Graduating Class:	
Position:	
Phone Number:	
Message to the Next Athlete:	

Name:	
Graduating Class:	
Position:	
Phone Number:	
Message to the Next Athlete:	

Name:	
Graduating Class:	
Position:	
Phone Number:	
Message to the Next Athlete:	

Name:	
Graduating Class:	
Position:	
Phone Number:	
Message to the Next Athlete:	

Name:	
Graduating Class:	
Position:	
Phone Number:	
Message to the Next Athlete:	

ABOUT THE AUTHOR

Hi There, I'm Richie Contartesi…**The founder of Next Play.**

And I understand firsthand the frustrations, challenges, and **aspirations** both you and your athlete are facing.

Like your athlete, I had a **dream of earning a college football scholarship** and was overlooked by everyone.

No one initially responded to my emails, DMs, or calls. I even had a meeting scheduled in person with a coach and **they didn't show up**.

However, at just **5'7" and 150 pounds**, I faced the adversity of being undersized and ultimately ended up created all of the systems you will find in this playbook.

After implementing the playbook, I defied all expectations and secured a full Division-1 **football scholarship** in the powerhouse South Eastern Conference (SEC) at Ole Miss.

I experienced the thrill of starting in all 12 games during my senior year, earned the prestigious **SEC Scholar Athlete award**, and played on legendary fields like Alabama, LSU, and Auburn.

My journey continued beyond college as I played **professional Arena football** and authored the #1 bestseller, "In Spite of the Odds." I even had the honor of being featured in the movie "Rudy Ruettiger: The Walk On."

But my true calling emerged when I founded Next Play. A nationwide mentorship program where I help **high school football players transcend their limitations** and secure college football scholarships using this playbook.

Today, I transform high school football players into confident communicators, leaders, and businessmen, so they can secure the best possible offers.

Drawing from my own journey and the success of athletes all over the country, I offer accountability, **mentorship**, and the proven systems needed to make their dreams a reality.

You and your athlete will discover a community where **89% of our athletes** secure football scholarships, and that understands, supports, and believes in their extraordinary potential.

instagram.com/richiecontartesi
x.com/richcontartesi
youtube.com/@richcontartesi

END NOTES

PLAY 1: THE CRITICAL FIRST STEP

1. Division 1 FBS: With 136 programs, each allowed up to 105 scholarships, the total number of scholarships available is 136 × 105 = 14,280.

   Division 1 FCS: With 110 programs (excluding Ivy League and Pioneer Football League), each allowed up to 63 scholarships, the total number of scholarships available is 110 × 63 = 6,930.

   Division 2: With 165 programs, each allowed up to 36 scholarships, the total number of scholarships available is 165 × 36 = 5,940.

   NAIA: With 95 programs, each allowed up to 24 scholarships, the total number of scholarships available is 95 × 24 = 2,280.

   29,430 scholarships / 1,100,000 HS players

   Divide the number of scholarships by the number of high school players:

   29,430 ÷ 1,100,000 = 2.6754545%

   Total D1 Scholarships: 14,280 + 6,930 = 21,210 divided by 1.1 Million = 1.9281818%

Made in the USA
Middletown, DE
14 November 2025